PARABLES *of the* GOSPEL

PARABLES *of the* GOSPEL

ST. GREGORY THE GREAT

Translated by NORAH BURKE

CLUNY

Providence, Rhode Island

CLUNY EDITION, 2023

This Cluny editon is a republication of the 1960
Scepter Press edition of *Parables of the Gospel*.

For more information regarding this title
or any other Cluny Media publication,
please write to info@clunymedia.com, or to
Cluny Media, P.O. Box 1664, Providence, RI 02901

VISIT US ONLINE AT WWW.CLUNYMEDIA.COM

ISBN (PAPERBACK): 978-1685952624
ISBN (HARDCOVER): 978-1685953058

NIHIL OBSTAT: Thomas F. O'Reilly, *Vic. Gen.*
IMPRIMATUR: Joannes Carolus, *Archiep. Dublinen, Hiberniae Primas*
DUBLINI DIE 3 MAR. 1960

Cover design by Clarke & Clarke
Cover image: Isaac Claesz van Swanenburg,
Parable of the Weeds Among the Wheat,
between 1590 and 1610, oil on panel
Courtesy of Wikimedia Commons

CONTENTS

FOREWORD

ONE DAY, beside the fishing boats on the shores of the lake of Genesareth, through the busy cities of Galilee, among the hills and barren hollows of the land of Juda… passed the Rabbi from Nazareth. He had never studied at the feet of the great masters of Israel, nor attended the lessons of the learned rabbis in the shade of the Temple porch; and yet Jesus, the son of Joseph the carpenter (Matt. 13:55), preaches to the people of Palestine, outdoes the arguments of scribes and pharisees and—most wonderful of all—"does not speak as the other teachers, but as one having authority" (Matt. 7:29). As he passes on his way no heart remains indifferent: some love him, others hate him with rage and fury. The master from Galilee delights in spending long hours with the crowds, explaining the message of salvation and teaching them about the kingdom of God, which is at hand.

The Son of Man, with a delicacy of condescension which can only be divine, adapts his discourse to the mental capacity of his hearers who, with the tempting morsel of his parables, swallow the hook of doctrine. How much he tells them of the kingdom of heaven. His most faithful disciples will retain it all, engraved upon their memory and their heart, until death. In time some of them, by a particular inspiration of the Holy Ghost, will write down many of the actions and words of the Master which the apostles—and especially Peter—have been repeating verbally in their preaching. And the disciples of the disciples, from one generation to another, will transmit to us the beating of the God-Man's heart, in the ever-vivid pages of the Gospel.

Jesus seasons his doctrine with parables which please and impress the simple people. But these parables, like a delicious fruit which never loses its savor, will retain their relish for the loving analysis of the centuries, to give freshness and vigor to our lips, light and hope to our impoverished intelligence.

Among the disciples of Jesus' disciples, the Fathers have left us a rich treasure in their commentaries on the parables of Our Lord. Outstanding among these commentaries are the homilies of Pope St. Gregory, from whose homiletic writings we have made the present selection.

Someone has happily defined the Gospel parables as "a prolonged comparison used by Our Savior for the purpose of teaching a truth of the supernatural order connected with the kingdom of God."

The parable, like the allegory, is born of comparison. A

comparison unites two terms by means of a particle, or a verb, or both: "Juda is like a roaring lion." The parable is the development of a comparison by means of a fictitious narrative for didactic purposes. The Gospel parables very often begin with an express formula of comparison: "The kingdom of heaven is like…," for example, a treasure hidden in a field. Here, in the parable, the comparison is developed and is not restricted to two terms, rather it compares two situations: that of the kingdom of heaven and that of the hidden treasure. But, unlike the allegory, in the parable each one of the narratives retains its own original meaning: the hidden treasure means hidden treasure, to which the kingdom of heaven is compared. If we were to strip the secondary term of the comparison of its own proper sense, substituting a figurative one, we would convert the parable, as it were, into an allegory. Therefore the parable keeps within the limits of the proper sense of a narrative; on the other hand the allegory belongs to the sphere of the improper sense, in effect, to the metaphorical.

But, at times, the two situations compared have a deep and suggestive correspondence. Think, for example, of the parable of the unruly vine-dressers:

> *A certain man planted a vineyard and let it out to husbandmen; and he was abroad for a long time. And at the season he sent a servant to the*

husbandmen, that they should give him of the fruit
of the vineyard. Who, beating him, sent him away
empty. And again he sent another servant. But
they beat him also and, treating him reproach-
fully, sent him away empty. And again he sent the
third; and they wounded him also and cast him
out. Then the lord of the vineyard said: What shall
I do? I will send my beloved son. It may be, when
they see him, they will reverence him. Whom,
when the husbandmen saw, they thought within
themselves, saying: This is the heir. Let us kill him,
that the inheritance may be ours. So, casting him
out of the vineyard, they killed him. What, there-
fore, will the lord of the vineyard do to them? He
will come and will destroy the husbandmen, and
will give the vineyard to others. (Luke 20:9–16)

On reading this parable, who can fail to see a figurative representation of the religious history of the people of
Israel? Who does not see the prophets of Yahweh in the
servants sent to gather in the fruits of the vineyard and,
finally, Our Lord—the Son of God—in the son of the owner of the vineyard, cast out and murdered by the husbandmen? In reality, here we are considering a parable in which
the two terms of comparison have a very deep relation: they
are not, so to speak, two disconnected narratives. The story

of the vine-dressers is also an allegory of the history of God and his chosen people. We see, then, that this is a mixed parable which is at the same time an allegory.

As a didactic means of expounding doctrine to the people the parable is clearly useful, as much for its power to arouse interest as for the impression it makes upon the memory. Once the anecdote makes an impact upon the latter, the correlated doctrine would seem to be indelibly engraved. Therefore, dealing with simple people, Our Lord often used this most effective oratorical method. Moreover, the Gospel parable, because of the depth of its content, gives ample scope for further investigation and applications with each new commentary. This is why it has always been an inexhaustible source from which we can extract the riches of Jesus' message.

Having said all this, it will be well to speak very briefly of our author. St. Gregory the Great was one of the last brilliant lights of the patristic era proper. He was born in Rome about the year 540. He belonged to an illustrious patrician family. Like many others of the Fathers, he abandoned a political career in early manhood, just when fortune was smiling on him. He renounced the praetorship of Rome, he disposed of his abundant wealth—which he gave to the poor and other charities—and converted his ancestral home upon mount Celio into a monastery, where he retired to the silence of the cloister following the discipline of the rule of St. Benedict.

But he was not to remain for many years in such peace. Like Ambrose, before he left the world, he had given evidence of a special aptitude for political affairs, in the same way as he also showed himself a humble and observant monk. So the Holy See called for his services without delay, and he, convinced that this was the will of God, returned to public affairs, very much against his inclinations, but resolved to defend the interests of the church and souls. Within a short time he was raised to the dignity of cardinal. Soon he went to Constantinople as Apostolic Nuncio, a most difficult and delicate mission, owing to the political enmities between the two capitals of the dismembered Roman empire. In 590 he was elected Pope, and died in 604.

St. Gregory, like all good Romans, was a man of practical genius, as seen from his difficult diplomatic missions and in his wise and fatherly government of the church. This same genius appears also in his writings, in which he shows special preference for pastoral, moral and canonical themes, intermingling dogmatic teaching with ascetical exhortation.

His literary works can be reduced to two essential groups: the Homilies and the Dialogues. These latter are a collection of spiritual considerations; they were written probably in 593 and 594. At this time Gregory, after some years of arduous work in the government of the apostolic See, allowed himself a temporary retirement to reorganize his interior life; his intimate companion was his friend the deacon Peter. The two spoke together of spiritual things and helped one another in the love of God, in ambition for sanctity and in charity for their fellow-men. From time to time Gregory would summarize these conversations, giving them a literary form.

The Homilies are composed of three series: twenty-two homilies on Ezechiel, forty upon different passages of the Gospels—*Homiliae in Evangelia*, and a book of Morals.

The doctrine of St. Gregory the Great has many points in common with that of St. Augustine: perfection does not absolutely exclude little faults due rather to intrinsic human limitations than to lack of good will; love of God and of our neighbor holds a predominant place in his writings; love is essentially active and must show itself in deeds; he analyses temptation and gives wise advice as to how we should behave when tempted.

But a unity and center shines through the whole of St. Gregory's ascetical doctrine: Christ. He perceived fully the responsibility of his ministry as shepherd of souls and to this object mainly he directs his writings, which are usually the fruit of his own preaching. He directs all his efforts to instructing the faithful in the ways of Christian perfection. He does not address any specific group of persons but, nearly always, the ordinary faithful; at times he reminds his priests of their mission, and furnishes them with doctrine so that they may guide the rest. Among pastoral duties he insists upon preaching and fraternal correction, loving but responsible, which the ministers of God must make to all classes of persons, according to their abilities, but without yielding to timidity, cowardice, human respect or false prudence.

We should have to write more pages than we wish if we were to attempt even an outline of the multiform work of St. Gregory the Great in the fourteen years of his pontificate. Let it suffice to add to what has been said already, that the Holy Father laid the foundations of the temporal domain of the church, that is to say of the *Patrimonium Petri* of the Roman See. Generously he met the social and economic calamities which the invasions of the barbarians produced in his time. He protected Rome from the Longobardi whom, finally, he guided towards Catholicism. He sent missionaries to England and strengthened relations with France and the Spanish visigoths. His skill was exercised in diplomatic battles with Constantinople. He reorganized ecclesiastical and liturgical discipline: from him derives the revision of church singing, called for this reason *Gregorian chant.*

PARABLES *of the* GOSPEL

I.

The Hidden Treasure

HOMILIA XI IN EVANGELIA

The kingdom of heaven is like unto a treasure hidden in a field. Which a man having found, hid it; and for joy thereof goeth and selleth all that he hath and buyeth that field. Again the kingdom of heaven is like to a merchant seeking good pearls. Who, when he had found one pearl of great price, went his way and sold all that he had and bought it. Again the kingdom of heaven is like to a net cast into the sea and gathering together of all kind of fishes. Which, when it was filled, they drew out; and, sitting by the shore, they chose out the good into vessels, but the bad they cast forth. So shall it be at the end of the world. The angels shall go out and shall separate the wicked from among the just; and shall cast them into the furnace of fire. There shall be weeping and gnashing of teeth. Have ye understood all these things? They say to him: Yes. He said unto them: Therefore every scribe instructed in the kingdom of heaven is like to a man that is a householder, who bringeth forth out of his treasure new things and old. (MATTHEW 13:44–52)

THE KINGDOM of heaven, dearly beloved brethren, is compared to earthly things, so that our soul may rise to the unknown from that with which it is familiar: so that by things which we see, we may find ourselves drawn to that which is unseen and, encouraged by daily experience, our love for what we know may kindle and inflame our desires for what we do not know as yet. Consider, then, that the kingdom of heaven is compared to a treasure hidden in a field, "which a man having found, hid it; and for joy thereof goeth and selleth all that he hath and buyeth that field." In all this, we should note that the treasure, once found, is hidden in order to preserve it; because the desire of celestial happiness is not sufficient shield against the evil spirits for him who does not hide it from human flattery. In this present life we are, as it were, in progress along a way which leads to our native land. As we go on our way the malignant enemies, like robbers, attack us. Therefore he who carries a treasure openly along his way, is anxious to be robbed. I say this, not that our neighbor should not see our works, as it is written: "That they may see your good works and glorify your Father who is in heaven" (Matt. 5:16), but so that we should not seek praise for what we do before others. Our exterior actions should be done in such a way that our intention remains hidden: in this way our good deeds set an example for our neighbor; but our intention—which is what pleases God—is that they remain unknown. The treasure stands for heavenly desires and the field in which this treasure is hidden signifies the conduct by which we achieve them. Then this field is bought by him who, selling all he has and renouncing the pleasures of the flesh, restrains his earthly desires, observing the divine instruction so that he delights in nothing which delights the flesh, while his soul shrinks from nothing which mortifies his carnal life.

We are told also that the kingdom of heaven is like a merchant in quest of good pearls who, having found one of great value, sells all he has and buys it; because he who attains a perfect knowledge of the heavenly life as far as this is possible, is supremely happy to relinquish all he loved before. In comparison with that sweetness nothing is of value, and the soul abandons all it had gained, scatters all it had amassed. Aflame with love for the things of heaven, it cares for nothing upon earth and considers as deformed all that once seemed so beautiful, for in the soul shines only the splendor of that priceless pearl. Of this love Solomon says: "Love is strong as death" (Canticles 8:6), because, as death strips the body of life, so love of life eternal kills the love of temporal things. He who is perfectly possessed of this love is as if insensible to earthly yearnings.

Not even the saint whose feast we celebrate today could have died for God as to her body if she had not died first interiorly, to terrestrial desires. Her soul, resplendent in its virtue, made little of torture and despised reward: led before armed tribunals she remained firm, stronger than the executioner, loftier than the judge. What have we to say to this, strong and robust men, when we see frail girls pass by means of the sword to the heavenly kingdom: we who are dominated by anger, puffed up with pride, disquieted by ambition and stained by impurity? And if we cannot reach heaven by suffering persecution, at least we should feel ashamed at not following God by peaceful paths. To none of us now does God say: Die for me. But he does say: Kill in yourself, at least, unlawful desires. If then, we do not wish to dominate the impulses of the flesh, how could we give life itself, should persecution come?

The kingdom of heaven is further compared to a fishing-net cast into the sea, gathering together all kinds of fishes, which, when it is full, is drawn to the shore where the good fish are selected to be kept and the bad to be thrown aside. Holy church is compared to a fishing-net, because she also is entrusted to fishermen and by means of her we are drawn out of the waves of this world and brought to the heavenly kingdom lest we be swallowed up in the abyss of everlasting death. She gathers together all classes of fishes because she offers pardon for sin to wise and ignorant, to free men and slaves, to rich and poor, to strong and weak. Hence the psalmist says to God: "All flesh shall come to thee" (Ps. 64:3). This fishing-net will be filled completely when it encloses the whole human race. It will be drawn out and the fishermen will sit beside it on the beach because, as time is represented by the sea, the shore signifies the end of time. At the end of time, the good fish will be separated and retained, while the bad will be cast out: because the good will be received into eternal rest and the wicked, having lost the light of the interior kingdom, will be cast into outer darkness. At present we mingle, good and bad together, like the fishes in the net; but the shore will tell us what was in the net, that is, our holy church. The fish which have been brought to shore have no further opportunity to change; but we are now in the net, wicked as we are, so that we may become good. Let us think well, brethren, while the fishing is still going on, so that we may not be rejected upon the shore. See how agreeable to you is the feast of this day, so that any of you who cannot assist at it feels no slight annoyance. What will a man do, then, on that day, when he is cast from the presence of the judge and deprived of the company of the elect, thrust from the light into eternal flames? This same comparison our Lord explained in a few words when he said: "So shall it be at the end of the world. The angels shall go out and shall separate the wicked from among the just; and shall cast them into the furnace of fire. There shall be weeping and gnashing of teeth." These words, dear brethren, are rather to be feared than to be explained. We are told clearly of the punishment that awaits sinners, lest anyone should offer his ignorance as an excuse if the eternal torments were spoken of in an obscure fashion. That is why Christ insists: "Have ye understood all these things?" And they answered: "Yes."

The concluding words of today's Gospel are: "Therefore every scribe instructed in the kingdom of heaven is like to a man that is a householder, who bringeth forth out of his treasure new things and old." If we understand, by the new and old which are mentioned, the two Testaments, we cannot admit that Abraham was instructed, since, although he knew the facts of the Old and New Testament, he did not announce them in words. Neither can we compare Moses to the householder because, although he explained things referring to the Old Testament, he did not expound the matter of the New. Therefore, since this explanation of these words is denied us, we must seek another. From the words of Truth Itself: "Every scribe instructed is like a householder," we can understand that it is not only those who did belong to the church who are signified, but those too who might have belonged, who bring to light new things and old when, through their words and actions, they reveal to us the preachings of both Testaments. It can be understood also in another way. The old destiny of the human race was to descend to the pit of hell in everlasting chastisement of sin. But the coming of the Mediator brought a new remedy, so that he who perseveres in doing right may merit entrance into heaven, and man, brought forth from the slime of the earth, may perish from this corruptible life to win a place in heaven. The old order, then, is: that, for its fault, mankind should suffer an eternal death; and the new: that it should be converted and enjoy celestial life. So that what our Lord says at the conclusion of his discourse is certainly what he had said at the beginning. First he compares the kingdom of heaven to a hidden treasure and to a precious pearl; then he speaks of the pains of hell and of the fire which consumes the wicked; and to conclude he adds: "Therefore every scribe instructed in the kingdom of heaven is like to a man that is a householder, who bringeth forth out of his treasure new things and old": as if to say in effect: The instructed preacher in our holy church is he who can say new things of the delights of the kingdom of heaven and recall old things which concern the terror of punishment, so that this latter at least may intimidate those who are not attracted by the reward. Let each man, then, listen attentively to what he is told of the heavenly kingdom which he must love, of the torments he must fear, so that if desire of heaven does not draw him, at least dread may move the sluggish soul, still clinging stubbornly to earth. Consider then, what we are told of hell: "There shall be weeping and gnashing of teeth." Since present joy is followed by eternal remorse, let us flee here, brethren, all vain gaiety, if hereafter we do not wish to weep. No one can rejoice here with the world, and reign hereafter with Christ. Restrain the desire for temporal delights and tame the impulses of the flesh. Whatsoever seems amusing in this present world the thought of undying fire suffices to embitter. Whatever diverts the untutored mind must be corrected by stringent discipline: that while we flee these worldly things of our own free choice, we may win with ease those lasting joys, through our Lord Jesus Christ.

II.

The Laborers in the Vineyard

HOMILIA XIX IN EVANGELIA

The kingdom of heaven is like to an house-holder who went out early in the morning to hire laborers into his vineyard. And, having agreed with the laborers for a penny a day, he sent them into his vineyard. And, going out about the third hour, he saw others standing in the market place idle. And he said to them: Go you also into my vineyard and I will give you what shall be just. And they went their way. And again he went out about the sixth and ninth hour and did in like manner. But about the eleventh hour he went out and found others standing. And he saith to them: Why stand you here all the day idle? They say to him: Because no man hath hired us. He saith to them: Go you also into my vineyard. And, when evening was come, the lord of the vineyard saith to his steward: Call the laborers and pay them their hire, beginning from the last even to the first. When therefore they were come that came about the eleventh hour, they received every man a penny. But, when the first also came, they thought that they should receive more; and they also received every man a penny. And, receiving it, they murmured against the master of the house, saying: These last have worked but one hour; and thou, hast made them equal to us that have borne the burden of the day and the heats. But he answering said to one of them: Friend, I do thee no wrong. Didst thou not agree with me for a penny? Take what is thine and go thy way. I will also give to this last even as to thee. Or is it not lawful for me to do what I will? Is thy eye evil, because I am good? So shall the last be first and the first last. For many are called but few chosen. (MATTHEW 20:1–16)

THIS PASSAGE of the holy Gospel calls for considerable explanation, which, lest I should burden your attention, I shall make as brief as possible. The kingdom of heaven is compared to a householder who hires laborers to work in his vineyard. Whom can this householder represent if not our Creator, who governs all those whom he made, who is master of his elect in this world as a householder is master of the servants in his house? He is owner of the vineyard, that is, the universal church which, from the just Abel to the last of the elect to be born at the end of the world, has produced many saints, like so many vine-branches. This householder sends workers to his vineyard in the morning, at the third, sixth, ninth and eleventh hours, because from the beginning of the world to the end he has not failed to send teachers to instruct the faithful. The morning of the world was from Adam until Noah: the third hour from Noah to Abraham: the sixth from Abraham to Moses: the ninth from Moses to the coming of Jesus Christ and the eleventh from the coming of Christ until the end of the world. At this last hour he sent the apostles who, coming so late, nonetheless received the full reward. God has never ceased to send laborers to instruct the faithful, as it were to cultivate his vineyard: for first through the patriarchs, then through the prophets and doctors of the law and lastly through the apostles, according as he gradually perfected the conduct of his people, he has labored in his vineyard. Yet anyone who lives in good faith and with a right intention can be considered, to a greater or lesser degree, as a laborer in this vineyard. The worker of the first hour, of the third, the sixth and the ninth, represents the ancient Hebrew people who, while they honored and revered their God with purity of heart, persevered in the cultivation of the vineyard from the beginning of the world. At the eleventh hour the gentiles have been called with these words: "Why stand you here all the day idle?" For these, so long after the creation of the world, still did not work for their living and were, so to speak, standing all the day idle. Meditate well, brethren, on their reply to this question: "They say to him: Because no man hath hired us." No patriarch had come to them, nor any prophet. And what do these words mean: No man hath hired us, but no one has preached the paths of life to us?

What shall we say in our own excuse, if we do not work, we who received our faith simultaneously with our birth, who have heard the words of life from our cradle, who drank the milk of heavenly teaching from the breasts of our holy church before our mothers had weaned us?

We may also apply these diverse hours to the different ages or stages in the life of every man. The morning of our intelligence is childhood. The third hour can be understood to mean adolescence, because when the sun climbs high in the heavens the heat of age increases. The sixth hour is youth because, like the sun which seems to have reached its zenith, in human life vigor is then in its plenitude. The ninth hour represents old age when, like the sinking sun, the fire of youth declines. The eleventh hour is what is called senility. As some are drawn to a good life in childhood, others in adolescence, others in youth, others in old age and some in decrepitude, it is as if the laborers were summoned at differing hours to the vineyard. Examine your behavior then, brethren, and see whether you are yet God's laborers. Let each one think over his conduct and see whether he is working in the vineyard of the Lord. He who in this life still searches for what is his own, has not yet entered God's vineyard. For only those are true workers of his, who consider his gain and not their own, who serve him with the zeal of charity and the desire to progress in virtue, watchful to gain souls for God and try to take others with them towards eternal life. But he who lives for himself, who feeds upon the luxuries of the flesh, is rightly reproached with his idleness since he does not tend the fruit of God's service.

He who neglects to live for God until he is nearing the end of his days stands idle, so to speak, until the eleventh hour. So that with good reason one may say to those who have been lazy all their lives: "Why stand you here all the day idle?" As if to say: "If you refused to live for God in childhood and in youth, at least repent in your last days before it is too late, and return to the path of Life when there is little time for labor left you." These the householder calls also, and in general rewards them before the others, because they leave this life to enter the kingdom sooner than those who appeared to be called from childhood. Was not the conversion of the good thief an eleventh-hour return, not on recount of his age but by the proximity of his death, when he professed belief in God upon the cross and breathed his last the next moment? The householder distributed the pennies beginning with the last worker who had entered the vineyard; for he brought the good thief, before Peter, to the repose of paradise. How many patriarchs there were before the announcement of the old law, how many afterwards, and nevertheless, those called to the kingdom of heaven at the coming of our Lord, arrived there without delay. Those who went to work at the eleventh hour received the same penny as those who worked from morning, because those who turn to God at the end of the world will receive the same reward of everlasting life as those who were called at the beginning. Hence the first who went to work said complaining: "These last have worked but one hour; and thou hast made them equal to us that have borne the burden of the day and the heats." The burden of the day and the heats has been borne by all those who, at the beginning of the world when men lived longer, had to endure more prolonged temptations of the flesh. To suffer the burden of the day and the heats is the same as to tire oneself through a whole lifetime, in the heat of one's flesh.

But we may ask: how is it said that they grumbled who themselves, although later, were called to the kingdom? No one who complains can enter the kingdom of heaven; no one who enters it can complain.

But as the fathers of old, who lived before the coming of Christ, were not brought to the kingdom by their holy lives alone, but by the death of him who opened the gates of paradise: their complaint would be that they lived a sanctity which merited heaven and nevertheless time passed without their entering it. Those who, after leading holy lives, went to the limbo of the just, can thus be said to have labored in the vineyard and complained; and one may say that those receive the same payment after their complaint who attain heaven having passed a long time in limbo. We who come to labor at the eleventh hour do not complain when we have worked, and we receive the penny; because we who are born into the world since the coming of our Mediator are brought to the kingdom as soon as we are freed from our body, and we receive that without delay which the fathers merited to enjoy only after a long time had passed. So the householder says: "I will also give to this last even as to thee." As the sharing of his kingdom is the fruit of the goodness of his will, he rightly adds: "Is it not lawful for me to do what I will?" It is foolish for man to complain of the benevolence of God. We cannot grumble if he does not give what he does not owe, but only if he fails to pay what is owing. So that Christ continues with striking aptitude: "Is thy eye evil because I am good?" Let no one be elated by his good works, nor by the length of time during which he has practiced them, when he hears the Truth pronounce this phrase: "So shall the last be first and the first last." See then that, although we know the number of our good works, we do not know how scrupulously the just judge will examine them. In any case we should rejoice exceedingly to be even the last in the kingdom of heaven.

And now what follows must inspire dread: "Many are called but few chosen," because many indeed are called to the faith but few reach the heavenly kingdom. See how many of us have gathered in this church to celebrate today's feast, we fill it to the doors; but who knows how few may be those who are counted among God's elect? We all acknowledge

Jesus Christ in word, but the lives of us all do not acknowledge him. The greater part follow God with their speech, but flee him with their conduct. This is what Paul means when he says: "They profess that they know God; but in their works they deny him" (Titus 1:16). And James says: "Faith without works is dead" (James 2:26). And the psalmist tells us: "I have declared, and I have spoken: they are multiplied above number" (Ps. 39:6). The faithful multiply above number at the call of our Lord, because sometimes they also receive the faith who are never counted in the number of the elect. Here they are mingled with the faithful by means of their confession, but because of their perverse life they do not merit to be counted in their number hereafter. This sheepfold which is our holy church intermingles sheep with goats; but, as the Gospel tells us, when the just judge comes, he will separate the good from the wicked, just as the shepherd divides the sheep from the goats (Matt. 25:32). For those who follow the pleasures of this world cannot be numbered in the kingdom among the sheep. There the just judge will separate the humble from those who are puffed up now with pride. They cannot receive the kingdom of heaven who, having received the gift of faith, labor assiduously in quest of the things of earth.

You see many of these in the church, of whom you must not despair although neither do you imitate their lives. We see what they are today, but we do not know what each one may be tomorrow. Sometimes he, whom we see follow us at a distance, will outstrip us in good works by industry and speed; and tomorrow we can hardly keep pace with him whom we seemed to excel but yesterday. When Stephen died for the faith, Saul kept the garments of those who stoned him; that is to say, Saul stoned him by the hands of all, because he enabled the others to throw the stones; and nonetheless in laboring for the church, he preceded even Stephen whom he had martyred. We should meditate, therefore, on two things above all others. The first is that, since many are called but few chosen, no one should feel sure of himself for, although he has been called to the faith, he does not know whether he is worthy of eternal life. The second is that no one should despair of his neighbor whom he sees, perhaps, plunged in vice, because no one can measure the depths of God's mercy.

I am going to speak to you, brethren, of an incident which occurred a short time ago, so that if you see yourselves in your hearts as sinners, you may have greater love for the mercy of almighty God. This very year a man came to my monastery, seeking admission: this monastery you know is situated near the church of the blessed martyrs John and Paul. He was respectfully received, and lived in an edifying manner.[†] A brother of his followed him to

---

†   *Dialogues*, book IV, chap. 38.

the monastery, but only corporally and not spiritually for, abhorring the life and the monastic habit, he lived in the monastery as a guest and refused to share the life of the other monks. He could not leave the monastery because, through lack of employment, he had not the means to live. His malice was burdensome to everyone, but all bore with him for the sake of his brother. He was proud and dissolute in his habits; he had no knowledge of an after-life, and mocked at those who tried to preach of it to him. He lived in the monastery in secular garb, was frivolous in his speech, restless, conceited, attentive to dress and dissipated in action. Last July he was stricken by the plague which you remember, and lay at death's door. He was at his last gasp, and life could be felt only in his breast and tongue. All the monks were present, praying God to grant him a happy death. But he, suddenly seeing a dragon coming to devour him, began to cry out in a loud voice, saying: "See how I am given over to be swallowed by a dragon, which cannot devour me because you are present. What are you waiting for? Go, so that I may be eaten up." When the monks advised him to make the sign of the cross, he answered as best he could: "I want to bless myself but I cannot, because the dragon is weighing me down. My face is covered with foam from his mouth, and his lips are suffocating me. See how he confines my arms; already my head is between his jaws." As he spoke thus, pale, trembling and almost dead, all the monks began to pray with greater fervor, seeking to assist the dying man by their supplications. Suddenly, freed from the oppression of the dragon, he cried: "Thanks be to God. The dragon which held me prisoner has disappeared, is gone, fleeing from your prayers." Then he made a vow to serve God and to become a monk. From that time onwards he endures fever and continual pains, for he was snatched from death, but not completely restored to life. As he was stained with serious and habitual guilt, he now suffers a continual infirmity; the life-giving fire of purification cleanses the hardness of his heart, for it is God's will that great malice should be purged by great affliction. Who would have believed that he was to be preserved and converted? Who can justly weigh the infinite mercy of God? At the hour of his death this wicked youth saw the dragon whom he had served all his life. The vision did not herald his death but was meant to show him whom he had served; that knowing he might resist, and resisting he might overcome. He saw him who had enslaved him while invisible to him, that seeing him he might win freedom thereafter. What tongue can extol sufficiently the wonders of God's mercy? What soul is not astonished on contemplating such great pity? Well had the psalmist considered the riches of God's clemency when he said: "Unto thee, O my helper, will I sing, for thou art God, my defense, my God, my mercy" (Ps. 58:18). So he who considered well the trials proper to this life calls God his helper, and since he receives us into eternal rest after we have passed through earthly afflictions, he also calls him his defense. But, remembering that God sees our wickedness, bears with our faults and nevertheless reserves rewards for us through penance, it was not enough for him to say that God is merciful, but he calls him mercy itself, saying: "My God, my mercy." Let us try, then, to remember all the evil we have done and the benevolence of God; let us consider the depths of his mercy, since not only does he pardon our faults, but promises the heavenly kingdom to those who repent of them. Then let each and all of us say, with all the ardor of our souls: My God, my mercy, who liveth and reigneth, threefold in unity and one in trinity, for ever and ever. Amen.

III.

The Marriage Feast

HOMILIA XXXVIII IN EVANGELIA

*And Jesus, answering, spoke again in parables to them, saying:
The kingdom of heaven is likened to a king who made a
marriage for his son. And he sent his servants to call them that
were invited to the marriage; and they would not come. Again
he sent other servants, saying: Tell them that were invited,
Behold, I have prepared my dinner; my beeves and fatlings are
killed, and all things are ready. Come ye to the marriage. But
they neglected and went their ways, one to his farm and another
to his merchandise. And the rest laid hands on his servants
and, having treated them contumeliously, put them to death.
But, when the king had heard of it, he was angry; and sending
his armies, he destroyed those murderers and burnt their city.
Then he saith to his servants: The marriage indeed is ready; but
they that were invited were not worthy. Go ye therefore into the
highways; and as many as you shall find, call to the marriage.
And his servants, going forth into the ways, gathered together
all that they found, both bad and good; and the marriage was*

filled with guests. And the king went in to see the guests; and he saw there a man who had not on a wedding garment. And he saith to him: Friend, how earnest thou in hither not having on a wedding garment? But he was silent. Then the king said to the waiters: Bind his hands and feet, and cast him into the exterior darkness. There shall be weeping and gnashing of teeth. For, many are called, but few are chosen. (MATTHEW 22:1–14)

I REMEMBER telling you on various occasions that in the holy Gospel the Church is frequently called the kingdom of heaven, a phrase which describes the assembly of the faithful. For, since God says through the prophet: "Heaven is my throne" (Isa. 66:1), and Solomon says: "Wisdom… conveyeth herself into holy souls" (Wis. 7:27), and Paul says also: "Christ, the power of God and the wisdom of God" (1 Cor. 1:24); it is clear that, if God is wisdom and the soul of the just man is the seat of wisdom, since heaven is said to be the throne of God, it follows that the soul of the just man is heaven. So that the psalmist says of the holy preachers: "The heavens show forth the glory of God" (Ps. 18:2). Then the kingdom of heaven is the church of the elect, because as in their heart they covet nothing of what exists on earth, longing only for what lasts for ever, God reigns in them as in heaven. This is why we are told: "The kingdom of heaven is likened to a king who made a marriage for his son."

Your great love already makes you understand who is

this king, father of a kingly son, namely: he of whom the psalmist says: "Give to the king thy judgment, O God: and to the king's son thy justice" (Ps. 71:1). And he arranged the marriage of his son. For God the Father gave God the Son in marriage, when he united him to human flesh in the womb of the Virgin; when he willed that he who was God in eternity should become man in time. But although a marriage takes place between two people, far be it from us to think that the person of the God-Man, our Redeemer Jesus Christ, is formed of two persons. We say that he exists of and in two natures: but we must be careful not to hold, for it is not true, that he is formed of two persons. We can say, then, with greater clarity and assurance, that the Father gave his royal son in marriage in as much as he united him to our holy church by the mystery of the Incarnation. The womb of the blessed Virgin Mary was the wedding-chamber of this bridegroom: so that the psalmist says: "He hath set his tabernacle in the sun: and he, as a bridegroom coming out of his bride-chamber" (Ps. 18:6). He did so when, in order to unite the church to himself, he took flesh in and came out of the most chaste womb of our Lady. And then he sent his servants to invite his friends to the marriage feast. He sent more than once, because he made known the Incarnation of Christ, first through the prophets and later through the apostles. Twice he sent his servants to summon all to the wedding, since he foretold the incarnation of his only-begotten Son by means of the prophets; and afterwards, by the apostles, he announced its accomplishment. But as those first who were invited did not wish to attend, when God issued the second invitation he says: "Behold, I have prepared my dinner; my beeves and fatlings are killed, and all things are ready."

The Gospel continues: "But they neglected and went their ways, one to his farm and another to his merchandise." In practice, to devote ourselves too much to the earthly and material side of our occupation is to see to one's farm, and we attend to our merchandise when we anxiously seek and covet the profit which derives from it. Since it is true that the person who gives himself completely to material tasks and he who dedicates himself exclusively to business matters both neglect to contemplate the mystery of the Incarnation, failing to harmonize their conduct with it, it follows that they resemble those men, going to their farm or their merchandise, who refuse to attend the marriage. It often happens, and this is much more serious, that some not only reject the grace which is offered to them, but even persecute the messenger. As we see when our Lord adds: "And the rest laid hands on his servants and, having treated them contumeliously, put them to death. But, when the king had heard of it, he was angry; and sending his armies, he destroyed those murderers and burnt their city." He destroys the homicides, that is, he kills those who persecute his servants. He burns their city; for not only the soul of such people, but also the body in which it dwells, is tormented in the everlasting flames of hell. It is said that the armies sent by the king destroyed his enemies, because God always executes his judgments by means of angels. What are those troops of angels but the armies of our king? This is why we call him God of *Sabaoth,* because *Sabaoth* means armies. He sends his army, then, because God takes his vengeance through his angels. The severity of that vengeance was preached to our ancestors in former times, and now we are witnesses to it ourselves. Where are those proud persecutors of the martyrs? Where now are those who rose up in arrogance against their Maker, puffed up with pride in the few fleeting glories of this world? See how the death of the martyrs bears fruit in the faith of those who are alive today; while, on the contrary, no one celebrates the memory of those who gloried in oppressing them. From the facts, then, we know what we are told in the parables.

But the king, his invitation slighted, wishes nevertheless to fill his son's wedding feast. He sends his servants to summon others, because even if some refuse to listen, God's word will always find a home at last. So that we read: "Then he saith to his servants: The marriage indeed is ready; but they that were invited were not worthy. Go ye therefore into the highways and the byways; and as many as you shall find, call to the marriage." If the word "highways" of which the evangelist speaks is interpreted as meaning our actions, here then, "byways" signify defects in our actions, or deviations from our way: for generally those come readily to God who find no prosperity in worldly affairs.

The Gospel continues: "And his servants, going forth into the ways, gathered together all that they found, both bad and good; and the marriage was filled with guests."

The quality of the guests shows us clearly that this marriage of the king represents the present church, where the wicked mingle with the good. In fact, the church is made up of her very many and very different children, because although she is the mother of all those who profess the faith, there are some whose vices prevent her from leading them to conversion of life and the liberty of grace. As long as we live on earth we must journey together, the good together with the bad. We shall be distinguished only when we reach the end of our journey. Thus the elect are never alone, except in heaven; neither are the wicked, except in hell. But this life, which hangs between heaven and hell, since it is between both, is filled indifferently by citizens of both quarters. The church receives them now indiscriminately to separate them later when they are leaving. Therefore, if you are good, you should bear patiently, while you are on earth, with those who are not. He who does not tolerate the wicked shows by his own intolerance that he is not really good. He who will not suffer the malice of Cain refuses the role of

Abel. Thus in the threshing, the grains are crushed among the chaff, flowers bud amid thorns and the rose breathes abroad its perfume from the midst of piercing briers. The first man had two sons, one of them belonged to the elect while the other was rejected (Gen. 4:1). Noah brought three sons with him in the ark: two of them were chosen and the last a reprobate (Gen. 7:7). Abraham had two sons: one was just while the other was disowned. (Gen. 11:10ff.). Two sons were born to Isaac, one just and the other made a castaway (Gen. 27:37). Jacob had twelve sons, one of them was sold in his innocence, the others sold him because they were wicked (Gen. 37:28). Twelve apostles were chosen: but one failed in the trial and eleven passed the test (John 6:71). The apostles ordained seven deacons (Acts 6:5); six of them persevered in the true doctrine but the seventh was the author of a heresy (Rev. 2:6).

Thus in the Catholic Church the good cannot be found without the wicked nor the wicked without the good. So, brethren, remembering these examples, resolve to bear with sinners; for if we are children of the just, we must follow in their footsteps. We cannot call that man good who refuses to tolerate those who are not so. So that the saintly Job says of himself: "I was the brother of dragons, and companion of ostriches" (Job 30:29). And Solomon says of the church, in the words of the Spouse: "As the lily among thorns, so is my love among the daughters" (Canticles 2:2).

Again, God speaks to Ezechiel and says: "O son of man...
thou art among unbelievers and destroyers, and thou dwellest with scorpions" (Ezech. 2:6). St. Peter glorifies the life of
blessed Lot, saying that God "delivered just Lot, oppressed
by the injustice and lewd conversation of the wicked; for in
sight and hearing he was just, dwelling among them who
from day to day vexed the just soul with unjust works" (2
Pet. 2:7). This is the reason why the apostle Paul praises and
commends the lives of his disciples, when he says: "That
you may be blameless and sincere children of God, without
reproof, in the midst of a crooked and perverse generation;
among whom you shine as lights in the world, holding forth
the word of life" (Philip 2:15). And John, speaking to the
church of Pergamus, writes: "I know where thou dwellest,
where the seat of Satan is. And thou boldest fast my name
and hast not denied my faith" (Rev. 2:13). Having considered all these men, brethren, it is evident that there is no
good man who has not had to suffer the perversity of the
wicked. The sword of our soul, so to speak, loses its keen-
ness if it is not sharpened upon the injustice of others.

It should not disquiet you in the least that in the church
there may be a large number of wicked people and few who
are good; for the ark which floated on the waters of the del-
uge in which we see an image of the church, was very wide
lower down, and narrowed with its height, since the apex
did not measure more than a cubit. We may suppose that

the lower part housed the quadrupeds and reptiles, while in the top lived birds and men. It was broader where the beasts were gathered; but where the men lived it was narrower, because in our holy church there are many who are carnally-minded, while those who value spiritual things are few. Where the church tolerates the perversities of men, it is as if her womb expands, but where she contains spiritually-minded men, she rises towards heaven and, since they are few, she becomes narrower. Because: "wide is the gate and broad is the way that leadeth to destruction; and many there are who go in thereat. How narrow is the gate and strait is the way that leadeth to life; and few there are that find it" (Matt. 7:13). The ark narrows at the top to a cubit's length, because in the church the more perfect its members, the fewer their number, and he alone reaches the summit who was born holy above all men and can be compared to no other. According to the expression of holy Scripture, he is "as a sparrow all alone on the housetop" (Ps. 101:8). One must tolerate the wicked, then, and all the more willingly in that they are so many; for, after the threshing, few grains remain to be stored in the granary and great heaps of straw are burned.

But now since by God's mercy you have entered the house where the marriage is taking place, that is to say holy church, see to it, dearly beloved brethren, that when the king comes he may have nothing with which to reproach you. We must think with fear and trembling of those words of the Gospel: "And the king went in to see the guests; and he saw there a man who had not on a wedding garment." What is meant, brethren, by this wedding garment? It cannot signify either baptism or faith, because who can enter this marriage feast without baptism or without faith? Because undoubtedly the mere fact of not believing excludes one from the church. So what can we understand by this wedding garment but charity? We must suppose, then, that this man enters without a wedding garment who is a member of our holy church by reason of his faith, but who lacks charity. It is so called with good reason because our Maker wore it when he came as a bridegroom to unite himself to the church. There was no other means than God's love by which the Only-begotten could unite the souls of the elect with himself. This is why John tells us: "God so loved the world, as to give his only-begotten son" (John 3:16). He who came to men for love's sake, calls this love the wedding garment. All of you, then, who are members of the church and believe in God have indeed come to the marriage, but you are without a wedding garment if you discard the cloak of charity. If any of you is invited to an earthly wedding, he changes his dress so that he may show the groom and bride his participation in their joy; he would be ashamed to appear shabbily-dressed among the guests and merrymakers. We assist at God's marriage feast and nevertheless, we are loath to undergo a change of heart. The angels rejoice when they see God's chosen ones admitted into heaven. How do we visualize this spiritual banquet, those of us who lack that festive garment which is the only one that gives us beauty in God's sight?

We must remember that, as a cloth is woven between two wooden frames, one above and the other below, thus also charity is founded on two precepts: the love of God and the love of our neighbor. For it is written: "Thou shalt love the Lord thy God with thy whole heart and with thy whole soul and with thy whole mind and with thy whole strength... and thy neighbor as thyself" (Mark 12:30; Deuteronomy 6:5). It is worth noting here that a limit and measure is set to the love of our neighbor, as we read: "Thou shalt love thy neighbor as thyself." The love of God, however, is marked by no limit, as we are told: "Thou shalt love the Lord thy God with thy whole heart and with thy whole soul and with thy whole mind and with thy whole strength." We are not told, then, how much we must love, but the manner in which we must do so: with everything we have. For only he truly loves God who does not think of himself. It is necessary to observe these two precepts of charity if we desire to be found wearing the wedding garment. This is what the prophet Ezechiel means when he tells us that the front of the gate of the city built on a mountain measures two cubits (Ezech. 40:9): for undoubtedly we cannot enter the heavenly city if in this church, which is called the gate because it is outside that city, we have no love for God or man. As we see also in the book of Exodus that it is prescribed that the curtains destined for the tabernacle should be dyed twice in scarlet coloring (Exod. 26:1). You, my brethren, you are the curtains of the tabernacle, veiling by virtue of your faith the heavenly mysteries in your hearts. But the curtains of the tabernacle must be twice dyed in scarlet. That is a color like fire: and what is charity, if it is not fire? But this charity must be twice dyed, that is, steeped in the love of God and in the love of our neighbor. The man who loves God so that his contemplation leads him to forget his neighbor has indeed the color of scarlet, but not twice dyed. Again, he who loves his neighbor, but whose love leads him to forget God, has the color of scarlet but with a single dye. In order that your charity may be steeped in both, you must be inflamed with love of God and of your neighbor, so that compassion for your fellow-man does not induce you to abandon contemplation of God, nor an excessive desire for that contemplation make you cast aside all pity. So, every man who lives among other men should seek God, the object of his longings, but in such a fashion as not to abandon his neighbor; and he should help his neighbor in such a way that it will never check his progress towards God to whom he speeds.

We know that the love which we owe to our neighbor is sub-divided into two precepts, as we read in Scripture: "See thou never do to another what thou wouldst hate to have done to thee by another" (Tob. 4:16), and Christ tells us: "As you would that men should do to you, do you also to them" (Matt. 7:12). If we act towards our neighbor as we should like him to act towards us, and avoid doing to others what would be displeasing to us ourselves, then we observe the law of charity. But no one should think that he observes this law merely because he loves his neighbor; he must examine first the motive behind his love. For he who loves others, but not for God's sake, has not charity, even though he may think he has. True charity lies in loving our friend with and in God, and our enemy for God's sake. He loves for God's sake, who loves even those by whom he is not loved. Charity is usually proved only by the opposing trial of hatred. So that our Lord says: "Love your enemies. Do good to them that hate you" (Luke 6:27). The man who loves his avowed enemies is following this command. Great and sublime are these precepts and often hard to obey; nevertheless they constitute the wedding garment. And that man who is without it has good grounds to fear that the king, at his coming, will cast him out. For we are told: "The king went in to see the guests; and he saw there a man who had not on a wedding garment." It is we, brethren, who attend the marriage of the Word: who believe in the church, are nourished by the Scriptures and rejoice in the union of God with the church. I would have you consider very carefully whether you attend the feast in the wedding garment. Weigh your actions in your heart one by one: whether you foster hatred of anyone, whether you envy the good fortune of others or through malice seek to injure them.

See the king entering the feast, see how he scrutinizes the disposition of our heart. To that man whom he finds stripped of charity, he says in rapid anger: "Friend, how earnest thou in hither not having on a wedding garment?" It is striking, dearly beloved, that he calls this man "friend" at the same time as he reproves him, as if his real meaning were: Friend and no friend; friend by faith and no friend by his actions. "But he was silent," since—with what pain we must say it—in that final judgment no word of excuse can help us, for he who accuses us outwardly is also he who accuses the soul's interior depths, who is a witness of our conscience. And yet we cannot forget that, if anyone has this garment of virtue, although not perfectly woven, he should not despair of obtaining the forgiveness of this merciful king when he comes, since he himself gives us this hope when he says through the psalmist: "Thy eyes did see my imperfect being, and in thy book all shall be written" (Ps. 138:16). We have said these words for the consolation of those who have charity, although weak. We must speak now of those who lack it altogether.

The Gospel continues: "Then the king said to the waiters: Bind his hands and feet, and cast him into the exterior darkness. There shall be weeping and gnashing of teeth." That rigorous sentence will bind the hands and feet of those who do not restrain themselves now from wicked actions by improving their life. In other words, suffering will bind hereafter those whom guilt binds here. The feet which refuse to visit the sick, the hands which refuse to help the needy, are now voluntarily unbound to any good works. Therefore the willing slave of vice here upon earth will hereafter be the unwilling prisoner of endless torments. It is apt to say that he is cast into the exterior darkness. Interior darkness is the blindness of the heart, while the exterior belongs to the everlasting night of damnation. That man is damned, then, who is banished into exterior, not interior, darkness for he is expelled against his will into the night of condemnation who, in this life, fell willingly into blindness of heart. It is said that there will be weeping and gnashing of teeth; the teeth of those who satiated themselves in their intemperance on earth will be set on edge in hell; their eyes will weep because in life they satisfied them with the sight of unlawful things. In this way, each member will suffer a particular torment as here it was used for the satisfaction of a particular vice.

But now that one man has been expelled, one who represents all the various types of evil, a general warning to all is given: "Many are called, but few are chosen." This is indeed a terrible sentence, my dear brethren. Consider that all of us have been called, by faith, to the marriage of the heavenly king. We all believe and confess the mystery of his incarnation, sharing in the banquet of the divine Word. But at a future date the king of judgment is to come. We know that we have been called; we do not know whether we have been chosen. It is all the more necessary, therefore, that we abase ourselves with humility, since we have not this certainty. There are some who never tried to do good; there are others who, although they began once, failed to persevere. We see one man pass nearly all his life in wickedness, but as he nears its end he returns to God by repentance and true penance. Another may seem to live the life of a saint, but end his days by falling into error and malice. One begins well and ends better; another plunges into evil from an early age and goes from bad to worse throughout his days. Each man, then, must live in fear, for he does not know what is to come, since we must never forget, but rather often repeat and meditate on the words: "Many are called but few are chosen."

IV.

The Ten Virgins

HOMILIA XII IN EVANGELIA

Then shall the kingdom of heaven be like to ten virgins, who, taking their lamps, went out to meet the bridegroom and the bride. And five of them were foolish and five wise. But the five foolish, having taken their lamps, did not take oil with them. But the wise took oil in their vessels with the lamps. And, the bridegroom tarrying, they all slumbered and slept. And at midnight there was a cry made: Behold, the bridegroom cometh. Go ye forth to meet him. Then all those virgins arose and trimmed their lamps. And the foolish said to the wise: Give us of your oil, for our lamps are gone out. The wise answered, saying: Lest perhaps there be not enough for us and for you, go ye rather to them that sell and buy for your-selves. Now whilst they went to buy the bridegroom came; and they that were ready went in with him to the marriage. And the door was shut. But at last came also the other virgins, saying: Lord, Lord, open to us. But he answering said: Amen, I say to you, I know you not. Watch ye, therefore, because you know not the day nor the hour. (Matthew 25:1–13)

I HAVE frequently exhorted you, dearly beloved brethren, to avoid evil actions, to preserve yourselves unstained by the corruption of this earth. But today's passage of the Gospel moves me to spur your vigilance in what concerns your good actions, lest in doing them, you seek some human gift or favor, for if you desire praise for your exterior actions, they merit no interior reward. Our Redeemer speaks of ten virgins: all are virgins, but not all enter through the gates of happiness; for some of them, who sought earthly esteem for their virginity, omitted to take oil in their vessels. But first we must ask: what does this kingdom of heaven signify and why it is compared to ten virgins who are called, moreover, foolish and wise? Since none of the wicked may enter that kingdom, why is it compared to the foolish as well as to the wise? We must know that often in holy scripture the kingdom of heaven represents the church militant. So that in another place Christ says: "The Son of man shall send his angels; and they shall gather out of his kingdom all scandals" (Matt. 13:41). In that kingdom of the blessed there are no scandals, but only the fullness of peace is to be found. And again we read: "He therefore that shall break one of these least commandments and shall so teach men shall be called the least in the kingdom of heaven. But he that shall do and teach, he shall be called great in the kingdom of heaven" (Matt. 5:19). Whoever preaches what he does not practice violates the commandment he would have others obey. That man is not worthy to enter the kingdom of eternal happiness who does not fulfill his own teaching. How then can he be called the least in the kingdom if he cannot even gain admittance? We must therefore understand that it is the present church which is signified here. In the church that teacher is called the least who breaks its precepts: contempt for his teaching must naturally follow upon scorn for his way of life. Each person has five senses which, multiplied by two, gives ten. Since the multitude of the faithful consists of persons of both sexes, the church is said to be like ten virgins. Here the good and the wicked, the elect and the rejected mingle, so that the similitude of wise and foolish virgins is justified. There are many who are chaste, restraining their desires for outward things and desire only an interior life; they mortify their bodies; full of an ardent longing for their heavenly home they refuse all human praise and seek eternal reward alone. These do not allow their glory to appear on men's lips, but hide it deep in their consciences. So also there are many who afflict their bodies by abstinence, but expecting to win thereby the esteem of others; they give good doctrine to others and give many alms. Nevertheless, these are foolish virgins, seeking only the fleeting reward of human praise. Apt, then, are those words: "But the five foolish, having taken their lamps, did not take oil with them. But the wise took oil in their vessels with the lamps." The oil represents the brightness

41

of glory, the vessels are our hearts, in which we carry all our thoughts. The prudent virgins had oil in their vessels because they kept hidden in their consciences the luster of this inward glory, as Paul asserts when he says: "our glory is this: the testimony of our conscience" (2 Cor. 1:12). The foolish virgins did not take oil with them because they did not hide their glory within, but sought it from their neighbors' lips. Note that all of them had lamps, but not all had oil: frequently the wicked can show good works just like the elect, but only those meet the bridegroom with oil who desire none but God's esteem for those outward actions. So that the psalmist says of the holy church of the elect "All the glory of the king's daughter is within" (Ps. 44:14).

"And, the bridegroom tarrying, they all slumbered and slept," for, since the judge delays his coming until the final scrutiny, both good and bad all sleep the sleep of death: for to sleep means to die. To slumber before one sleeps signifies the decline of health: growing infirmity lulls us into the sleep of death. "And at midnight there was a cry made: Behold, the bridegroom cometh. Go ye forth to meet him." A cry at midnight announces the arrival of the bridegroom: thus the day of judgment is so hidden in obscurity that we cannot know beforehand when it will come. It is written: "The day of the Lord shall so come as a thief in the night" (1 Thess. 5:2). Then all the virgins awake, because both good and wicked are roused from the sleep of death.

They trim their lamps, that is, they count the number of their good works in reward for which they hope to receive eternal happiness. But the lamps of the foolish virgins fail, because their works, which were seen so clearly by men, wane and vanish at the coming of the judge. From God they will receive no recompense, for men gave them the praise they esteemed so highly. What are we to understand by that petition for oil which they make to the prudent virgins if not that, in the hour of judgment, discovering their interior want, they seek testimony from without? As if, deceived by their own presumption, they said to their neighbors: "Since you see us rejected as if we had done no good works, tell what you have seen of them." But the wise virgins answer: "Lest perhaps there be not enough for us and for you." For in that day (I say this of some who rest in the peace of the church) the testimony of each one will scarcely suffice for himself: how much less, then, for him and for his neighbor? So that immediately they are exhorted: "Go ye rather to them that sell and buy for yourselves." The sellers of oil are the flatterers. For they who, when anyone receives grace from God, attribute its luster to his merits, act as if they sold oil. Of this oil the psalmist says: "Let not the oil of the sinner fatten my head" (Ps. 140:5). The head is the principal part of the body, and here it signifies the soul, which governs the body. The oil of the sinner fattens our head when the applause of the flatterer gratifies our soul. "Now whilst

43

they went to buy the bridegroom came": because while they seek a witness to their lives from their neighbor, the judge comes, who is witness not only of their works, but of their heart. "And they that were ready went in with him to the marriage. And the door was shut."

Ah, if only we could realize with all our heart the wonder of those words: "the bridegroom came"! What sweetness when "they went in with him to the marriage"! What bitterness when "the door was shut." He will come, indeed, whose coming petrifies the elements, in whose presence the earth and heavens tremble. So that he says by the prophet: "Yet once more; and I will move, not only the earth, but heaven also" (Haggai 2:7, Hebrews 12:26). All the human race will undergo that scrutiny. He who is served by angels, archangels, thrones, principalities and powers comes to chastise the wicked, to remunerate the good. Think, brethren, what will be the terror of that day, in the presence of such a judge, when there will be no escape from his judgment. What confusion that man will feel who, for his faults, must blush before the assembly of angels and men. What fear to see him in anger whom the human mind fails to understand even when he is quite serene. Thinking of that day the prophet says: "That day is a day of wrath, a day of tribulation and distress, a day of calamity and misery, a day of darkness and obscurity, a day of clouds and whirlwinds, a day of the trumpet and alarm" (Zephaniah 1:15). Consider dearly beloved with what bitterness he foresaw that day of judgment, since so many phrases will not explain it. How the blessed will rejoice in their recompense, when they enjoy that vision of him in whose presence the elements tremble and they will go in with him to the marriage. At the same time as they rejoice in the nuptials of the bridegroom, they themselves will be the bride: for in the bridal chamber of the eternal kingdom they are united for ever to their God. Thenceforth that vision can never be snatched from their possession. The door of the kingdom will close for ever upon those left outside, who then will weep; that same door is now open to all penitents. There will be repentance then, but it will be fruitless: they will not find pardon then who waste the time now in which they might repent. So that Paul says: "Behold, now is the acceptable time; behold, now is the day of salvation" (2 Cor. 6:2). And the prophet says: "Seek ye the Lord while he may be found: call upon him while he is near" (Isa. 55:6).

The Lord does not hear the virgins call him, because once the door of the kingdom is closed they can no longer approach him, who was formerly so approachable. Thus the parable adds: "At last came also the other virgins, saying: Lord, Lord, open to us. But he answering said: Amen, I say to you, I know you not." The man who does not heed God's precepts cannot merit to have his petition heard; he who wasted the time of fruitful penance pleads in vain before the gate of the kingdom. So God tells us through Solomon: "Because I called, and you refused. I stretched out my hand, and there was none that regarded. You have despised all my counsel, and have neglected my reprehensions. I also will laugh in your destruction, and will mock when that shall come to you which you feared. When sudden calamity shall fall on you, and destruction, as a tempest, shall be at hand: when tribulation and distress shall come upon you. Then shall they call upon me, and I will not hear: they shall rise in the morning and shall not find me" (Proverbs 1:24ff.). Hear them plead that the door be opened, sadly invoking the name of the master; goaded on by the anguish of their rejection they cry: "Lord, Lord open to us." They pray, but their prayers are not heard: for God will abandon as unknown to him those whom he does not now recognize, by the merit of their lives, as his own. It is right, then, that he should give his disciples this general counsel: "Watch ye, therefore, because you know not the day nor the hour." Since repentance can blot out sin, if a man foresaw the hour of his death he could devote some of his time to pleasure and the rest to penitence. But God, who has promised pardon to the penitent, has not promised another day on earth to any sinner. Therefore we must be in continual fear of that last day whose date we cannot foresee. Reflect that we have been given this very day on which we are speaking in order to make a truce with God and be converted: nevertheless we refuse to lament the evil we have done. Not only do we not repent of the evil committed, but we even increase the guilt for which in justice we should weep. But if any illness attacks us, if its symptoms indicate the approach of death, then indeed we ask for a prolongation of our life in order to bemoan our sins, we pray with all our heart and soul. Yet when we are well we act quite otherwise.

I am going to tell you, brethren, a story whose consideration will be of great profit to you if you listen with attention. In the province of Valeria there was a man named Chrysorius, commonly called Chryserius: a talented man, but with as many vices as possessions: puffed up with pride, dominated by passion and becoming more and more a slave to avarice. But God, determined to put an end to so much wickedness, afflicted him with an illness. I have heard this from a saintly person who is still alive, a relative of this man. Lying at the point of death, on opening his eyes, he saw black and fearsome spirits come towards him, to drag him down to hell. He began to tremble and grow pale and he broke out in a cold sweat. In the hope of respite he called for his son Maximus, a monk known to me personally; and he cried with vehemence: "Quickly, Maximus, for I have never done you any wrong. Take me under your protection!" Soon Maximus arrived, much perturbed, and all the family gathered, weeping and trembling. They could not see the evil spirits which he saw menacing him,

47

but they felt their presence in his confusion, his shuddering and his pallor. Driven by terror of these horrible phantoms, he turned himself this way and that in the bed; lying on his left side he could not bear the sight of them: turning to the wall they were there before him. So that in despair of ever freeing himself from these dreadful visions, he cried aloud: "A truce until tomorrow, a truce until tomorrow." But in the act of uttering these words, he died. So it is clear that he had this vision for our sake, not for his own: that what he saw should be of profit to us for whom the divine patience is still waiting. For in what way could it benefit him to see those foul spirits before his death and to seek a truce, when it was not granted him? We should consider this example earnestly, dear brethren, lest our time go by in vain and we should have to seek longer life to do good works, when the time comes for us to leave this mortal body. Remember our Lord's words: "Pray that your flight be not in winter or on the sabbath" (Matt. 24:20). According to the precept of the old Law (Exod. 16), it was forbidden to walk a great distance on the sabbath-day and the winter also is a time unsuitable for travelling, because the cold hinders our steps. He says then, "Pray that your flight be not in winter or on the sabbath," as if to say: "See that you do not wish to fly from your sins when it is no longer permissible to travel." Now, while we may, let us think of that time when the possibility shall end. We should have the thought of our death constantly before our minds, remembering this counsel of our Redeemer: "Watch ye, therefore, because you know not the day nor the hour."

V.

The Talents

HOMILIA IX IN EVANGELIA

*For even as a man going into a far country called his servants
and delivered to them his goods; and to one he gave five talents,
and to another two, and to another one, to every one according
to his proper ability; and immediately he took his journey. And
he that had received the five talents went his way and traded
with the same and gained other five. And in like manner he that
had received the two gained other two. But he that had received
the one, going his way, digged into the earth and hid his lord's
money. But after a long time the lord of those servants came and
reckoned with them. And he that had received the five talents,
coming, brought other five talents, saying: Lord, thou didst
deliver to me five talents. Behold, I have gained other five over
and above. His lord said to him: Well done, good and faithful
servant, because thou hast been faithful over a few things, I will
place thee over many things. Enter thou into the joy of thy lord.
And he also that had received the two talents came and said:
Lord, thou deliveredst two talents to me. Behold, I have gained*

other two. His lord said to him: Well done, good and faithful
servant: because thou hast been faithful over a few things, I will
place thee over many things. Enter thou into the joy of thy lord.
But he that had received the one talent came and said: Lord, I
know that thou art a hard man; thou reapest where thou hast
not sown and gatherest where thou hast not strewed. And, being
afraid, I went and hid thy talent in the earth. Behold, here thou
hast that which is thine. And his lord answering said to him:
Wicked and slothful servant, thou knewest that I reap where
I sow not and gather where I have not strewed. Thou oughtest
therefore to have committed my money to the bankers; and at
my coming I should have received my own with usury. Take ye
away therefore the talent from him and give it him that hath
ten talents. For to every one that hath shall be given, and he
shall abound: but, from him that hath not, that also which
he seemeth to have shall be taken away. And the unprofitable
servant cast ye out into the exterior darkness. There shall be
weeping and gnashing of teeth. (MATTHEW 25:14–30)

THE READING of this Gospel, dearly beloved, would have us
consider that those of us who receive more gifts than others
in this world, will be judged more strictly by its Creator. For,
according as the gifts increase, the account demanded will
be more exacting; therefore a man should be more humble
and use his gift more diligently in God's service, the more
heavily he sees himself indebted. Here, then, is a man about

to set out on a journey. He calls his servants and distributes some talents among them, so that they may trade with
them. After a long time he returns to ask those servants
for an account of their doings. He rewards those who have
worked well and gained profit but he condemns the slothful
for ever. Who is this man who sets out on a journey, but
our Redeemer, who ascended into heaven in that same flesh
which he had assumed? The earth is the proper home of the
flesh, but it travels, as it were, to foreign lands, when our
Redeemer ascends with it to heaven. This man, on the eve
of his journey, entrusted his goods to his servants because
he left spiritual gifts to the faithful who believed in him. To
one he gave five talents, to another two, and to another only
one. There are five senses of the body: sight, hearing, taste,
touch and smell; so the five talents represent the gift of the
five senses: that is to say, external knowledge. The gifts of
understanding and action are signified by the two talents,
and the single talent represents the understanding alone.
But he who received the five talents gained another five, for
there are some people who, although they cannot understand interior and mystical things, nevertheless, by their
desire for their heavenly home, teach sound doctrine to all
whom they meet, doctrine concerning those exterior matters which they can understand. As they themselves refrain
from the caprices of the flesh, they are freed from the fetters of earthly things and from the desire of visible delights,

and by their counsel, they free others also. Likewise, there are some who as if endowed with two talents, have a good grasp of what refers to intellect and action: they understand the subtleties of the interior life, and outwardly they work wonders. When they teach others by their learning and example they derive, as it were, a double profit from their trading. But he who received only one talent, going his way, made a hole in the ground and hid his master's money. To hide one's talent in the earth is to occupy the intelligence God gives us in purely earthly matters, not to seek spiritual profit, never to lift our heart above worldly considerations. For there are some who received the gift of understanding, but who, nevertheless, understand only the flesh. Of these the prophet says: "They are wise to do evil, but to do good they have no knowledge" (Jer. 4:22). But our Lord, who gave the talents, returns to demand an account of them, for he who now, in mercy, distributes spiritual gifts, will examine each one's merits in a severe judgment: he will compare what each received with the gain he has derived.

The servant who returned double the talents he had received is praised by his lord and is awarded an everlasting prize as he hears his master say: "Well done, good and faithful servant, because thou hast been faithful over a few things, I will place thee over many things. Enter thou into the joy of thy lord." Paltry are the goods of this world, however great they may seem, in comparison with that reward of eternal life. But the faithful servant is placed over many things when, the afflictions of corruptible life overcome, he rejoices in the eternal delights of that celestial home. Then he is admitted to the perfect happiness of his lord, when he is taken to that everlasting dwelling, to mingle with the assembly of the angels and to relish that joy in such a way that he can never more suffer the external pains of temporal distress.

The servant who was unwilling to trade with his talent returns to his lord with an excuse, telling him: "Lord, I know that thou art a hard man; thou reapest where thou hast not sown and gatherest where thou hast not strewed. And, being afraid, I went and hid thy talent in the earth. Behold, here thou hast that which is thine." We should note that the worthless servant says that his master is hard, and nevertheless he refuses to serve him; he says that he was afraid to trade with the talent he was given, when in fact he should fear its profitless return to his master. This servant is a figure of many in the church, who are afraid to lead a better life, but not afraid to continue in the quagmire of their inertia; because they consider themselves to be sinners, they tremble to approach the way of sanctity, but they are not afraid to persist in their vices. And Peter himself, as yet weak in his faith, resembled these Christians when he said on seeing the miraculous draught of fishes: "Depart from me, for I am a sinful man, O Lord" (Luke 5:8). If you consider yourself a sinner, for that very reason you will do well not to repulse Christ from you. But they who find an excuse for evading a conversion and returning to a better way of life because they consider they lack faith, who call themselves sinners and repel that master who could instruct them in sanctity, are like madmen who cannot use their intelligence, for they are dying and still in mortal dread of Life. So that this servant receives a speedy answer: "Wicked and slothful servant, thou knewest that I reap where I sow not and gather where I have not strewed. Thou oughtest, therefore, to have committed my money to the bankers; and at my coming I should have received my own with usury." The servant is convicted by his own words when his lord says: "I reap where I sow not and gather where I have not strewed." If, according to your own judgment, I demand what I have not given, how much more justly will I demand of you what I gave you to put to profitable use? You should have given my money to the bankers and, on returning, I would have received my money with interest. To give money to the bankers is to give the knowledge of preaching to those who can exercise it.

As you see the risk I run, brethren, if I misuse my Master's talent when preaching to you, consider also the danger you yourselves are in, for he will demand an account, and with interest, of these things which you now hear. You know how usurers receive over and above what they have lent: when we return them what they gave us we must add some money which we were never given. Remember, then, that you must pay interest for the words you hear, trying with what you hear to understand what is not said. You must learn, by following your inner conscience and deducing one thing from another, to perform yet more than that to which the preacher exhorted you. But listen to the sentence passed upon the idle servant: "Take ye away therefore the talent from him and give it him that hath ten talents."

It would have seemed more natural to give the talent taken from the worthless servant to him who had received two talents rather than to him who had received five, that is, to him who had less rather than to him who had more. But, as we said before, by the five talents the five senses are signified, that is to say the knowledge of exterior things, while the two talents represent understanding and action. Then he who had received the two talents had more than him who received five because the latter, who merited the praise of his master by his stewardship of the exterior things he had been given, was as yet without the interior gift of understanding. The one talent, then, representing intellect, was rightly given to him who looked well to his outward responsibilities. We see this occur every day in the church: many who are faithful servants in external things, who put to profitable use the outward benefits which God's grace confers on them, attain a mystical understanding which produces also their inward enlightenment.

Immediately we hear that other sentence which is passed upon mankind in general: "To every one that hath shall be given, and he shall abound: but, from him that hath not that also which he seemeth to have shall be taken away." It will be given to him who already has and he shall abound, for everyone who has the gift of charity receives other gifts besides. But he who has not the gift of charity will lose even those gifts which he seemed to have. So it is necessary, brethren, that charity should be the motive of all your actions. It is true charity to love your friend in God, and your enemy for God's sake. He who has not charity loses all the good he had; he is deprived of the talent he was given and, in the words of Christ himself, he is cast into exterior darkness. The punishment of him who voluntarily lived in interior darkness is to be thrust into exterior darkness; there against his will he must suffer the darkness of punishment because here he willingly enjoyed the blindness of his passion.

We should observe that no idler is completely deprived of talent. There is no one who can say truly: I have received no talent and therefore I cannot be called to account for it. We have all received something, however small, for which we shall have to render an account. One receives the gift of intelligence, and with it the duty of preaching. Another receives worldly wealth, and with it the obligation of using it well. Another receives neither intelligence nor wealth but he learned the craft with which he earns his livelihood, and this same skill will be accounted to him as the talent given. A fourth possesses none of these things, but it chances that he enjoys the friendship of some rich man, and this familiarity is his talent. If he neglects to mediate with his friend on behalf of the poor, he is condemned for burying his talent. To sum up: let him who has intelligence speak out boldly; he who has riches must be untiring in works of mercy; he who has a profession or art should exercise it in the service and the profit of his neighbor; he who enjoys the friendship of an influential person should fear condemnation for his indolence if he does not make intercession on behalf of the poor. The judge, when he comes, will demand from each of us in accordance with the gifts he gave us. So that each one may be sure that his account will be an acceptable one he should think continually, and with fear, of the gifts he has received. For now the time is near when he who left us will return. For when he, having been born on this earth, went far away from it, it was as if he went on a journey; but soon he will return to call us to account. If we slacken in our good works, he will judge us all the more severely for those talents which he gave us. Think, then, of what you have received, and try to profit by its use. No earthly cares must distract us from spiritual works lest, if we hide the talent we have been given, we arouse the anger of the lord to whom it belongs. The slothful servant digs up the talent when the judge is already examining his faults, as there are many who leave earthly desires or actions behind only when they are cast into eternal punishment by the sentence of the judge. Let us watch, then, in the time left us before we have to account for our talent, so that when the judge approaches to condemn he may find excuse for us in the profit which we have made. May God grant us this, who lives and reigns, world without end. Amen.

VI.

The Sower

HOMILIA XV IN EVANGELIA

And when a very great multitude was gathered together, and hastened out of the cities unto him, he spoke by a similitude: The sower went out to sow his seed. And, as he sowed, some fell by the way-side, and it was trodden down; and the fowls of the air devoured it. And other some fell upon a rock, and, as soon as it was sprung up, it withered away, because it had no moisture. And other some fell among thorns; and the thorns, growing up with it, choked it. And other some fell upon good ground and, being sprung up, yielded fruit a hundredfold. Saying these things he cried out: He that hath ears to hear, let him hear. And his disciples asked him what this parable might be. To whom he said: To you it is given to know the mystery of the kingdom of God; but to the rest in parables, that seeing they may not see and hearing may not understand. Now the parable is this: The seed is the word of God. And they by the way-side are they that hear; then the devil cometh and taketh the word out of their heart, lest believing they should be saved. Now they upon the

rock are they who when they hear receive the word with joy; and
these have no roots; for they believe for a while and in time of
temptation they fall away. And that which fell among thorns
are they who have heard and, going their way, are choked with
the cares and riches and pleasures of this life and yield no fruit.
But that on the good ground are they who, in a good and perfect
heart, hearing the word, keep it and bring forth fruit in patience.
(LUKE 8:4–15)

THE LESSON of the holy Gospel which you have just heard,
my dear brethren, requires no explanation, but only exhortation. Since Christ himself explained it, human weakness
cannot dare to question his illustration of it; rather, you
must dispose yourselves to consider it carefully. If it were I
who told you that the seed signifies the word, the field the
world, the birds the demons and the thorns riches, perhaps
you could doubt my words: but it is our Lord himself who
interprets his own words so that you may learn to interpret
the significance of those things which he did not set forth
fully. At the outset he tells us that he is speaking metaphori-
cally, so that when our littleness grasps the figurative meaning of his words we may give our assent to his doctrine.
Who would ever credit me if I wished to interpret thorns as
riches, especially since thorns pain us, while riches delight
us? And yet these are thorns, because they wound our soul
with the prickings of the thoughts they inspire; by enticing

us to sin, they besmear us with their pollution like the blood from a wound. So that, in the words of another evangelist, he does not call them riches merely, but deceitful riches (Matt. 13:22). They are deceitful because they cannot remain with us for ever, they are deceitful because they cannot satisfy the needs of our heart. The only true riches are those which make us rich in virtues. So, brethren, if you wish to be rich, love true wealth; if you desire the highest honors, seek the kingdom of heaven. If you love the glory of high rank, hasten to be numbered among that exalted court of the angels.

Engrave upon your memory those divine words you have heard just now. The word of God is food for the soul, but it is as if our stomach were sick and rejected food if we hear the word but do not retain it. If a man cannot retain food in his stomach, his life is imperiled. You have to fear, then, the danger of an everlasting death, if you receive the food of this holy admonition, but do not retain the words of life, which are the food of the just man. Reflect that everything you do is passing away and that, willingly or unwillingly, each day hastens you towards the last judgment, and none of the time passed will ever be re-granted you. Why should we love what we must leave? Why do we neglect the end which we must certainly reach? Remember these words: "He that hath ears to hear, let him hear." All who were there listening to Christ had ears of the body. But he who said to those same people: "He that hath ears to hear, let him hear", was referring, beyond doubt, to the ears of the heart. See then that the discourse which you hear takes root in your heart. Take care that it does not fall by the wayside, lest the wicked spirit come and take it away. See that it does not fall on stony ground, and shoot up in good works without the roots of perseverance. Many are pleased by the things they hear, and they resolve to do good works, but as soon as difficulty arises they abandon what they had begun. The rocky ground had no moisture, for it did not bring to the fruit of perseverance the seed which sprouted in it. Many, when they hear a sermon against avarice, detest that vice and extol contempt of earthly goods, but as soon as the soul sees something it desires, it forgets what it once extolled. There are those also who, when they are admonished against impurity, not only do not desire to commit sins of the flesh, but are very ashamed of those which they have committed; but as soon as physical beauty tempts them, their heart is so carried away by desires that it is as if they had never resolved to oppose those desires. They fall then into serious sin, which they themselves had condemned on remembering their former guilt. Often we feel compunction for our faults and, nevertheless, once our lamentations are over, we return to those same faults. Thus Balaam wept over the tents of the Israelites, asking for a death similar to theirs when he said: "Let my soul die the death of the just;

and my last end be like to them" (Numbers 23:10), but as soon as the moment of compunction passed, he was burnt up by the vice of avarice. For the sake of the reward he was promised, he gave counsel for the destruction of this people upon whose death he wanted to model his own; he forgot all repentance and would not quench those covetous flames. We must note well what our Lord tells us, namely that cares, pleasures and riches smother the divine word. They smother it because they strangle the soul by their endless attacks: they prevent the entrance of good desires, and our soul languishes without the vital breath it needs. Consider also that there are two things joined with riches: temporal cares and pleasures; because riches oppress our mind with worry and weaken it with abundance. By an apparent contradiction they make their possessors both anxious and pleasure-seeking; but since pleasure cannot co-exist with anxiety, at times they afflict men with solicitude, and at other times, by their abundance, dissipate them in pleasures.

The good earth "brings forth fruit in patience," for the good works which we do are of no value if we will not suffer with patience the wicked actions of our neighbor. The higher we ascend, the harder things we will have to suffer, for as our love for this world weakens, its trials still increase. So that we often see many who are good, and who suffer many tribulations. They flee from all earthly desires, and still they meet with more severe afflictions. But, as our

Lord says, they bring forth fruit in patience, for if they bear this scourging with humility, they will find heavenly rest. Thus the grape is trodden, and gives its wine. So, also, the olive renders up the scum when it is pressed, and its juice becomes pure oil; and in the threshing-machine the grain is separated from the straw and, thus cleansed, is stored in the granary. Therefore if a man wishes to overcome his vices completely, then he must be careful to bear humbly the sufferings of his purification. Then he can hope to present himself unstained before the judge, his soul purified by the fire of tribulation.

In the porch of the church of St. Clement there was a certain man by the name of Servulus, known to many of you as well as to myself, poor in possessions and rich in merits, incapacitated by a long and painful illness, for from early years until the end of life he was a paralytic. I do not have to remind you that he could not even stand; he had never been able to sit up in bed, nor raise a hand to his mouth, nor turn from side to side. His mother and his brother attended him continually, and by their hands he distributed among the poor whatever alms he was given. He had never learned to read, but had bought the books of sacred scripture and used to have these read him by certain religious to whom he gave hospitality in his own house. In this way he had a complete knowledge of the scripture, as far as his capacity permitted, since, as I have said, he had never learned to read. He always sought, in the middle of his sufferings, to give God thanks and to bless and praise him day and night. But as the time drew near for so much patience to be rewarded, the pains of death attacked him. As he knew that death was near, he desired those pilgrims and others who had enjoyed his hospitality, to stand and sing some psalms with him as death approached. As they sang together with him, the dying man suddenly silenced their voices, crying out with a terrible voice: "Be silent, do you not hear these praises resound in heaven?" And as his heart listened to those melodies which he heard within himself, his saintly soul left his body. As it did so, such a fragrant perfume filled the place that those present were filled with unspeakable sweetness, so that it was clear that those voices he had heard were welcoming his soul to heaven. A monk of our monastery who is still alive was present at that occurrence, and he has attested frequently and with tears, that while the body remained unburied, the fragrance of that perfume remained. See how this man ended his life, who bore his sufferings with such patience. According to Christ's words, the good earth yields good fruit in patience: ploughed by hardship and severity it yields the harvest of reward. But I would have you ponder, brethren, what excuses we are to offer in that strict account which will be demanded of us, we who have received many gifts and the use of our members, and nonetheless are reluctant to perform good works, when one who was destitute of means and physical capacity carried out so faithfully the precept of our Lord. Let us not run the risk of the Lord contrasting us with the apostles, who brought so many multitudes of the faithful to heaven with them, through their preaching; or with the martyrs, who won their heavenly reward by shedding their blood. What defense shall we make then, when we see this Servulus of whom we spoke, his arms rendered useless by his long disease, which yet could not prevent his good works? Dearly beloved, seek to do many good works and so to imitate the good that, making them your model here on earth, you may be their companions in that kingdom which is to come.

VII.

The Harvest Is Great

HOMILIA XVII IN EVANGELIA

And after these things the Lord appointed also other seventy-two. And he sent them two and two before his face into every city and place whither he himself was to come. And he said to them: The harvest indeed is great, but the laborers are few. Pray ye therefore the Lord of the harvest that he send laborers into his harvest. Go: Behold, I send you as lambs among wolves. Carry neither purse, nor scrip, nor shoes; and salute no man by the way. Into whatsoever house you enter, first say: Peace be to this house. And, if the son of peace be there, your peace shall rest upon him: but if not, it shall return to you. And in the same house, remain, eating and drinking such things as they have; for the laborer is worthy of his hire. Remove not from house to house. And into what city soever you enter, and they receive you, eat such things as are set before you. And heal the sick that are therein and say to them: The kingdom of God is come nigh unto you. (LUKE 10:1–9)

OUR LORD and Savior, dearly beloved brethren, teaches us sometimes with his words and at other times with his actions. His acts themselves are indeed precepts, because when he does something even without speaking, he is showing us what we should do. Here you see that he sends his disciples out in pairs to preach; for the precept of charity is twofold, namely, the love of God and of one's neighbor, and charity cannot exist except between two persons. No one, properly speaking, can be said to have charity towards himself, because the object of love must be another person if it is to be called charity. Our Lord sends his disciples two by two in order to indicate to us tacitly that he who has not charity towards others, cannot possibly be given the task of preaching.

It is rightly said that "he sent them two and two before his face into every city and place whither he himself was to come." For truly our Lord follows his preachers; because doctrine prepares our mind, and then he comes into our soul after we have heard words of exhortation by which we are led to the truth: Hence God says to these preachers, through the mouth of Isaias: "Prepare ye the way of the Lord, make straight in the wilderness the paths of our God" (Isa. 40:3). To them also, the psalmist says: "Make a way for him who ascendeth upon the west" (Ps. 67:5). Christ ascends upon the west because although he surrendered himself in his passion and death, he manifests far greater glory by his resurrection. He ascends upon the west because, through his resurrection, he overcame the death which he had undergone. In preaching his glory to you, then, we are preparing a way for him who ascends upon the west so that later, when he comes, he may enlighten you by his love.

Consider what he says to the preachers whom he sends: "The harvest indeed is great, but the laborers are few. Pray ye therefore the Lord of the harvest that he send laborers into his harvest." There are few laborers to reap that plentiful harvest, a fact which must cause us sorrow; because although the words of justice find many hearers, there are few to speak them. There are many priests in the world, and still we find very few laborers in God's harvest, because we have received the sacerdotal charge but fail to fulfill its obligations. But consider deeply, brethren, what is said: "Pray ye therefore the Lord of the harvest that he send laborers into his harvest." Pray for us that we may serve you loyally, that our tongue may never rest from preaching, lest, having received this duty, our silence should accuse us before the just judge. Often the voice of preachers is silent through their own fault; often it is the fault of their subjects, who try to prevent them from speaking. The tongue of the preacher is mute through his own fault, as the psalmist says: "But to the sinner God hath said: Why dost thou declare my justices?" (Ps. 49:16) And sometimes the preacher is impeded from speaking by the vices of his subjects: as God said to Ezechiel: "And I will make thy tongue stick fast to the roof of thy mouth; and thou shalt be dumb, and not as a man that reproveth: because they are a provoking house" (Ezech. 3:26). As if he really meant: I take away from you the right of preaching, because this people has enraged me by its actions and does not deserve to be encouraged in the way of truth. It is hard to know whose is the fault when the preacher is silent: what we certainly know is that sometimes his silence prejudices himself, but always prejudices those who should hear him.

But, if we have not sufficient energy to fulfill our duty of preaching, at least let us preserve the innocence of life proper to the priestly consecration. Our Lord says: "Behold, I send you as lambs among wolves." There are many who, when they are given the task of ruling others, become hard and severe, to the great oppression of their subjects. They use their power to terrify and injure those whom they should assist. Since they lack true charity, they wish to play the part of masters, forgetting that it is their duty to act as fathers. They exchange humility for pride in the position which they occupy, and although outwardly they may chance to show indulgence, inwardly they remain fierce. Of them Christ says in another place that they come to you in the clothing of sheep, but inwardly they are ravening wolves (Matt. 7:15). We must remember, dearly beloved, that we are sent as lambs among wolves, and we must pro-tect our innocence, lest malice overcome us. He who occu-pies the preacher's pulpit, then, must inflict no evil; rather he must bear with evil, that by his very mildness he may soften the anger of the violent, and that, by his own distress at the afflictions of others, he may heal the wounds of sin. If on any particular occasion a proper zeal requires that he should exercise some severity with his subjects, this sever-ity should proceed from his love and not from harshness. In this way, as he gives external demonstration of the rights of his authority, inwardly he is filled with a fatherly love for those whom outwardly he chastises so severely. This is what our blessed Master taught us when he showed that his was no selfish love, desiring nothing of this world and never stooping to the yoke of any earthly ambition.

And he continues: "Carry neither purse, nor scrip, nor shoes; and salute no man by the way." Such confidence in God should the preacher have that, although he does not provide for the necessities of this life, nevertheless he is persuaded that he will never lack them. This precludes his spending the time in quest of temporal goods for himself which he should devote to procuring eternal goods for oth-ers. Nor is he allowed leisure for conversation along the way, to show us with what speed we must hurry along the path of preaching. These words can also be understood metaphor-ically: they can signify that money, which is usually carried in a purse, represents hidden wisdom. Then he who has wisdom of speech, but neglects to use it for the benefit of others, carries it, as it were, tied up in a purse. So that we read: "Wisdom that is hid, and a treasure that is not seen, what profit is there in them both?" (Sirach 41:17). And what else does the scrip represent, but the cares of this world? And do the shoes not signify the example of dead works? It is not fitting that he who undertakes the task of preaching should burden himself with worldly affairs, lest, engrossed in such matters, he forget the business of eternal life. He must not stop to consider the example of others' foolish conduct, thinking to improve his own works with such lifeless leather. There are many who try to defend their own wicked deeds by comparing them to the wickedness of others. As they have seen others do, they consider that they have a right to do also: is not this to act as if they sought to cover their feet with the skins of dead animals? He who salutes another along the way wishes him good health merely because he is on a journey, not through any real concern for the other's health. So he who preaches salvation to his hearers, not out of love for his eternal fatherland, but merely for the desire of the reward he wins for himself, acts as if he were saluting them along the way, desiring their salvation because of the circumstances, but not through any good will.

Christ continues: "Into whatsoever house you enter, first say: Peace be to this house. And if the son of peace be there, your peace shall rest upon him: but if not, it shall return to you." The peace offered by the preacher either rests on the house, if the peaceful man dwells there, or else returns to him again: because either there will be someone there predestined to eternal life, who follows the doctrine he hears; or, if no one wishes to listen, the preacher himself will not go unrewarded, because that peace returns to him, and God will recompense him for his labors.

Consider also that although our Lord forbade his disciples to carry purse or scrip when he sent them to preach, nevertheless, he allows them to have food and the necessities of life for that preaching. For he adds: "And in the same house, remain, eating and drinking such things as they have; for the laborer is worthy of his hire." If our peace is welcomed, it is fitting that we should remain in that same house, eating and drinking whatever we are given, that so we may receive temporal assistance from those to whom we offer the rewards of eternal life. So the apostle Paul, considering these earthly things of small importance, says: "If we have sown unto you spiritual things, is it a great matter if we reap your carnal things?" (1 Cor. 9:2). And we should think on what he says elsewhere: "The laborer is worthy of his reward" (1 Timothy 5:18). For material food is part of the preacher's reward, and in this way the payment of his wage is begun upon earth, to be completed in heaven with the everlasting vision of truth. It follows, then, that from one task which we fulfill we derive a double payment: one while still on our journey, another upon arrival; one to sustain us in our labors, another to reward us at the resurrection.

The returns we reap in this present life should strengthen us to aspire all the more to the heavenly prize which follows it. No one should preach in order to receive temporal remuneration, rather he should be remunerated in order to be able to preach. Anyone who preaches to obtain a reward either of praise or of profit most certainly loses that which is eternal. But the man who seeks to please others by his discourse in order that, while they enjoy his eloquence, the love of God, not love for that eloquence, may grow in them, or he who receives temporal assistance through his preaching so that necessity may not oblige him to curtail it: these will undoubtedly win that recompense in heaven, although they have accepted these supports along the way.

But what is to be said of those of us—it pains me even to ask this question—who reap the reward, but do not labor? We enjoy the fruits of our holy church by accepting our daily stipends, but we work little in our preaching of the eternal church. Let us consider what serious condemnation is merited by one who reaps the reward of work he never did. We live on the offerings of the faithful, but what do we do for the good of their souls? We accept the gifts they bring to the altar in reparation for their sins, but we do not strive as we should to eradicate those sins, either by our sermons or by our prayer. We hardly dare to practice Christian courage in rebuking anyone for his faults even (which is all the more serious) if it is a question of some person of influence in the world; perhaps we even extol those errors lest, if they be opposed, he should discontinue his former offerings. We should keep constantly in mind what has been written of some: "They shall eat the sins of my people" (Hos. 4:8). Why is it said that they shall eat the sins of the people, unless it means that they foster the sins of delinquents for fear of losing their temporal offerings? If we, who live upon the stipends of the faithful who bring them to the altar in reparation for their sins, eat and are silent, it is undeniable that we eat their sins. Consider, then, how serious a sin it is in God's eyes to eat the sacrifices of sinners and not to preach against their sin. Listen to the saintly Job: "If my land cry against me, and with it the furrows thereof mourn: if I have eaten the fruits thereof without money..." (Job 31:38–39). The land cries against its owner when the church complains, with justice, of its preacher. The furrows mourn if the hearts of his hearers, cultivated by his predecessors with the voice of doctrine and the rigor of their admonitions, see cause for lamentation in his way of life. The good owner does not eat the fruits of his land without money, that is without paying for them, for the wise preacher first pays his talent, which is his doctrine, so that he may not take from the church the unearned stipend which brings him condemnation. We eat the fruits which we have rightly bought when we accept the assistance of the faithful for whom we have labored in the work of preaching. We are the heralds of the judge who is to come, and who will announce his coming, if the preacher's voice be mute?

It must be clear then that, as far as each one can, as far as his energies will allow, he must endeavor to impress upon the flock committed to his care a certain tenor of that future judgment and the sweetness of the heavenly kingdom. He who has not the capacity to guide all of the faithful at the same time by means of a common exhortation, has the obligation of instructing them as well as he can individually: he must edify them in private conversation and with simplicity cultivate good fruits in the hearts of his children. We should think continually of those words spoken to the holy apostles and, through them, to us: "You are the salt of the earth" (Matt. 5:13). If we are salt, we must season the souls of the faithful. Those of you who are shepherds of souls must reflect that you are grazing the flock of God. Of his flock God says through the psalmist: "In it shall thy animals dwell" (Ps. 67:11). We often see that salt is given to animals, so that they may lick it and improve in health. The priest should be to the people what salt is to those animals; he must consider, then, what he must say to each, and how to admonish each, so that every one that converses with him, as meat sprinkled with salt, is seasoned with the taste of that life which will never end. But we are not salt of the earth if we do not season the hearts of those who hear us. This beneficial condimentation of his fellow-men is carried out only by him who is faithful to his task of preaching.

But we are true preachers of justice only if we put our preaching into practice, if we feel deep sorrow for having offended God whom we love, if we wash with our tears the daily blemishes in our human life, which no one can traverse without some fall or other. We shall feel real sorrow if we reflect upon the deeds of our predecessors, and derive contempt for our own life from the consideration of their glory. We feel true sorrow if we meditate on the precepts of God with attention and try to improve by following those commandments by which those others improved whom we now venerate. Thus it is written of Moses: "He made also the laver of brass, with the foot thereof, of the mirrors of the women that watched at the door of the tabernacle" (Exod. 38:8). Moses, indeed, erected a wash-basin of bronze so that the priests might wash before they entered the Holy of Holies: for the law of God commands us first to wash ourselves with sorrow, so that our filth may not render us unworthy to penetrate into the purity of his mysteries. It is aptly said that this basin was made from the mirrors of the women who watched continually at the door of the tabernacle. The mirrors of the women represent the precepts of God, in which saintly souls examine themselves ceaselessly in order to discover any stain of ugliness upon them. They correct any defects in their way of thinking or of living, just as one beautifies one's face by the reflection in a mirror: as they use all their energies in fulfilling God's commands, they recognize immediately what in them is pleasing to their heavenly bridegroom, and what in them displeases him. It is clear that as long as we are upon this earth we cannot enter the everlasting tabernacle. But the women watched at the door of the tabernacle because, although saintly souls are oppressed by the weakness of the flesh, nevertheless their love keeps a constant vigil at the entrance to eternal life. Moses, then, made a basin for the priests from the mirrors of the women, because the law of God offers the waters of sorrow for the stains of our sins, at the same time as it prescribes those same heavenly precepts for our fulfillment which made the saints fit to become spouses of God. These precepts, if we consider them attentively, reveal to us the blemishes of our soul; and seeing them, we are moved to sorrow; then it is as if we were washed in the basin made from the mirrors of the women. It is essential that, when we feel sorrow for our sins, we should feel great zeal for the lives of those committed to our charge. The pain of remorse should not distract us from vigilance for our neighbor. Of what profit is it if, loving ourselves, we abandon our neighbor? Of what use is it if, loving and caring for our neighbor, we neglect ourselves? In the old law (Exod. 25:4) it was prescribed that the cloth which adorned the tabernacle should be twice dyed in scarlet: so in the sight of God, our charity should have the twin coloring of love of God and love of our neighbor. He esteems himself rightly who loves his Maker with a pure heart. The cloth is twice dyed in scarlet, then, when the soul is inflamed with love for its neighbor and for itself, for the sake of him who is the Truth.

But in the midst of these considerations, we must always remember that it is our duty to exercise an upright zeal against the wicked actions of our neighbors, without allowing the heat of rebuke ever to make us forget the virtue of meekness. A priest's anger should not be hasty or passionate, but always softened by counsel and long reflection. We must bear with those whom we correct, and correct those with whom we have to bear: lest, if one of these elements be absent, the action of the priest be lacking either in zeal or in mildness. So we see that, in the building of the temple of old, its pedestals were commanded to be adorned with sculptures of lions and oxen and cherubim. The cherubim represent the fullness of knowledge. But why, in these pedestals or bases do the lions not appear without the oxen, nor the oxen unaccompanied by the lions? What do the bases represent, but the priests of the church? These, while the government of souls is entrusted to them, support like foundation-stones the burden laid upon them. The cherubim are depicted there, because it is essential that the priest should be adorned with all knowledge. The lion represents the terror of severity, while the patience of the meek is depicted in the ox. So it is that lions and oxen are always represented together, because in the priest, the virtue of mildness must always accompany the rigor of severity. Thus his gentleness will soften his anger; but the heat of reproval must inflame his meekness too, so that it may not lack efficacy.

But why do we speak of these things when we see that many are guilty of far greater crimes? I speak to you, bishops, with tears, because I know that some of you have ordained priests for money, have sold spiritual grace, and of the wickedness of others, by a damnable sin, you have reaped temporal profit for yourselves. Why do you forget Christ's words: "Freely have you received; freely give" (Matt. 10:8)? Why do we forget that when our Redeemer entered the temple he overthrew the chairs of the dove-sellers and scattered the money of the changers (John 2:14ff.)? Who are the sellers of doves in God's church today but those who receive payment for the imposition of hands? By those sacraments, the holy Spirit is called down from heaven. The dove is sold because the imposition of hands by which the Holy Ghost is received, is offered for a price. But our Redeemer overthrew the tables of those who sold doves: because he annuls the priesthood of those who so traffic in spiritual goods. This is the reason why the canons of the law condemn the sin of simony, and prescribe that those who seek money for the ordinations they make shall be deprived of their own priesthood. The tables of the dove-sellers overthrown, then, signify that those who sell spiritual gifts lose their priesthood either in the sight of God alone or also in the eyes of men. Indeed, there are many other evils committed by the pastors of the church, but which are hidden from human eyes. There are many who appear as saints before men, but who do not even blush to appear blackened and stained before the eyes of the interior Judge. The day will come, very soon, when the Pastor of pastors will come and make known the doings of each one; and he who now through his prelates chastises the faithful for their faults will then himself punish the wickedness of the prelates. So that, going into the temple, he made a whip of cords and casting out the evil traders from the house of God, overthrew the tables of those who sold doves: for he punishes through his pastors the faults of their subjects, but he himself chastises the corruption of the pastors. In this life our secret actions can be hidden from men, but that judge will come inevitably, from whom our silence will hide nothing, and who cannot be deceived by our denials.

There is something further, brethren, in the pastor's life, which weighs upon my mind. Lest perhaps my accusation arouse resentment, I must accuse myself also of this; although impelled as I am by the necessity of these barbarous times, I am an unwilling culprit. We have devoted ourselves to external things, and our actions show the distorted value we place upon the honor we have received. We abandon the task of preaching and, culpably in my opinion, we call ourselves bishops who are such only in name and not in practice. Those who are committed to our care may turn their backs on God, but we are silent. They grovel in evil actions, and still we do not stretch out our hand to correct them. They perish daily in their many sins, and we watch indifferently as they advance towards hell. But how are we to correct the lives of others, if we will not correct our own? Busied with temporal affairs, we become more insensible to interior urgings of grace, the more we concentrate on outward matters. By constant dealings with worldly cares, the soul becomes deaf to heavenly inspirations: as it becomes harder and harder by reason of its material actions, it cannot soften to the love of God. So that our holy church has said with truth of its ailing members: "They have made me the keeper in the vineyards: my vineyard I have not kept" (Canticles 1:5). The tending of our vineyard is our daily labor in the fulfillment of our ministry: but although we have been placed as guards over others' vineyards, we fail to tend our own because, busied with other occupations, we neglect the duties of our ministry. I believe, brethren, that God receives no offence so great as he does from priests who, placed by him in his church in order to correct others, set them instead the example of their own wickedness: when he sees sin committed by those who should curb sin. What is yet more grievous, and sometimes happens, is that priests, who should help others from what they have themselves, wrest from others all that they can. We also see them deride those who live in humility and continence. Think, then, what will be the fate of the flock when the shepherd himself becomes a wolf. For these are they who are given the task of caring for God's sheep: men who do not hesitate to exploit them: pastors against whom the flock itself must be on guard. We do not seek the good or advancement of their souls, but, devoting ourselves to our own affairs, we desire only worldly goods and are intent on earthly glory alone. Since we are meant to be leaders of the others we enjoy a greater liberty, and we turn our blessed ministry to the service of ambition. We abandon God's cause, and give ourselves to mundane matters; we accept the post of sanctity and involve ourselves in temporal business. In our own conduct we see fulfilled to the letter that saying: "And there shall be like people like priest" (Hos. 4:9). The priest does not differ from the people when his behavior shows no merit which excels theirs.

Let us implore the tears of Jeremias; let him consider our death and say weeping: "How is the gold become dim, the finest color is changed: the stones of the sanctuary are scattered in the top of every street" (Lamentations

4:1). The gold is dimmed because the life of the priest, once resplendent with the glory of his virtues, is seen now to deserve only blame for the vileness of his actions. The finest color is changed because the tunic of sanctity has been ignominiously defiled by low and despicable deeds. The stones were placed inside the sanctuary, and the high priest walked upon them only when he entered the Holy of Holies, probing the secrets of his Maker. We, brethren, are the stones of the sanctuary, who should be constant witnesses of the secrets of God, who must never take our gaze away from them: that is, to be occupied in worldly matters. But the stones of the sanctuary are scattered in the top of every street because those whose interests should lie with interior affairs and a life of prayer, dedicate themselves to a wicked pursuit of outward things. You see that now there is scarcely any secular calling with which priests are not occupied. Since their lives, like their sacred garb, are altogether external, they lie, like the stones, outside the sanctuary. As the Greek word here meaning street derives from the word for width, when we are told that the sanctuary-stones lie in the streets, this means that some religious follow the broad and spacious paths of the world. Not only are they scattered in the streets, but at the top of the streets, because they are ambitious for worldly enterprises, and still they seek in virtue of their religious habit to obtain the highest honors. They are scattered, then, at the top of the streets, because they lie inactive in the duties of their ministry and they desire to be honored for their semblance of sanctity.

You have seen how the sword of this world strikes; you see continuously how the people suffer chastisement. Why, if not because of our sins, do they suffer so? See towns decimated, strongholds overthrown, churches and monasteries destroyed, while lands lie deserted. We are the authors of the death of this people which is perishing, we who should bring them life. Through our sin many lie prostrate, because we have neglected to instruct them in the doctrine of eternal life. What are the souls of men but the food of God, created to be united with him to increase the everlasting church? But we must be the salt of that food. As we mentioned already, Christ told his disciples: "You are the salt of the earth." If the people are the food of God, the priests must season that food. But because we neglected to pray and to preach, the salt has lost its savor; it cannot season the food of God who therefore does not accept it, because our negligence has rendered it insipid. Let us ask ourselves whether there are any who have done penance, who have been converted by our preaching, dissuaded from evil actions by our reproval. Who has ever abandoned impurity at our exhortation, who has given up avarice, or who has renounced his pride? Let us think what profit we have gained in trading for God, we who have received our talent and been sent out by him, for the Lord said: "Trade till I come" (Luke 19:13). Remember that his coming draws near, and he will demand from us the profit of our labors. What profit, what improvement in souls, will we show him as gain from our dealings? What sheaf of souls will we present to him in that harvesting of our preaching?

Let us always keep before our minds the dreadful day of judgment, when the judge will come, and his servants must account for those talents which he entrusted to them. Then he will be seen in awful majesty, among the choirs of angels and archangels. Just and wicked will appear for this examination, and each one will be seen to be what his actions have made him. There we shall see the apostle Peter guiding the converted Jews who followed him; and Paul followed by the world which he won for Christ. Andrew will lead Achaia; John leading Asia and Thomas leading India: all will appear before their acknowledged king. We shall see then the shepherds of God's flock, with the numbers of souls which they bring after them to God by the force of their instruction and exhortation. When, on that day, all the shepherds lead their flocks to the eternal Shepherd, what shall we say, who return miserably empty-handed from our trading: we who bear the name of pastors and cannot show the sheep which have fed upon our doctrine? Here we are called pastors, but there we shall have no flock.

But, if we neglect the sheep, does God therefore abandon them? By no means. He himself leads them to pasture, as he promised through his prophet Ezechiel; for he instructs all those whom he has predestined to eternal life and hastens their steps by the spur of suffering and contrition of heart. By our ministry the faithful receive holy baptism; they are blessed by our prayers; by the imposition of our hands the Holy Ghost comes down upon them. So they reach the heavenly kingdom, while we, by our negligence, slide backward. The just man, cleansed by the absolution of the priest, enters heaven: while the priest, by his evil life, speeds to the pains of hell. To what can I liken bad priests? To the water of baptism which, blotting out the sins of those baptized, flows on into the sewer. Let us fear this disaster, brethren; let us act always as befits the dignity of the priesthood. Let us think daily of reparation for our sins lest our lives, by which God frees others, remain shackled to our guilt. Let us remember well what we are, what is our business, the charge we have received. We must learn to balance daily the account we shall have to settle with our judge. And we must so minister to ourselves as not to forget the welfare of others, so that none who comes in contact with us be left unseasoned by the salt of our conversation. When we see a person lead a licentious life, we should counsel him to seek in marriage a restraint for his passions, so that by what is lawful he may learn to conquer the unlawful. When we speak to a married man we should advise him to transact his temporal affairs in such a fashion that God's love still holds priority; and that, by pleasing his wife, he must not displease his Maker. When we have to deal with a cleric, we must admonish him to live in a manner which will be an example to lay people, lest through anything reprehensible in his behavior, our religion should be brought into contempt. When we see a monk, we should counsel him to respect the habit he wears, in his words, actions and thoughts; that he renounce completely the things of this world, and so attain by his conduct in the eyes of God what his garb makes him in the eyes of men. He who already is holy must be directed to make further progress; he who is wicked must be exhorted to correct his ways. All this so that no one who speaks to the priest may depart without the salt of his advice. Think diligently on these things and use the result of your meditation for the good of your neighbors. Prepare to give to God the fruits of your trading. All this I shall foster in you more effectively by praying than by speaking further.

Let us pray. O God, who hast willed to call us to be pastors of thy people, we pray thee that we may be in thy sight what men hold us to be. Through our Lord.

VIII.

The Barren Fig Tree

HOMILIA XXXI IN EVANGELIA

He spoke also this parable: A certain man had a fig tree planted in his vineyard; and he came seeking fruit on it and found none. And he said to the dresser of the vineyard: Behold, for these three years I come seeking fruit on this fig tree and I find none. Cut it down therefore. Why cumbereth it the ground? But he, answering, said to him: Lord, let it alone this year also, until I dig about it and dung it. And if happily it bear fruit; but if not, then after that thou shalt cut it down. And he was teaching in their synagogue on their sabbath. And, behold, there was a woman who had a spirit of infirmity eighteen years. And she was bowed together; neither could she look upwards at all. Whom when Jesus saw, he called her unto him and said to her: Woman, thou art delivered from thy infirmity. And he laid his hands upon her; and immediately she was made straight and glorified God. (LUKE 13:6–13)

Our Lord and Savior speaks to us through his Gospel sometimes with words and other times with actions; sometimes he tells us one thing in actions and quite another thing in words, and sometimes he tells us the same thing in both. You have heard, brethren, of two things in the Gospel of today: the barren fig tree and the deformed woman. And in both cases mercy is exercised. What he tells us in the parable he subsequently puts into action. For the barren fig tree signifies the same thing as the cripple; and the fig tree spared for another year is the same thing as the woman's body made straight. The owner of the vineyard came the third time to the fig tree and found no fruit on it, and the woman who was cured had been bowed together for eighteen years. The eighteen years during which the woman suffered her infirmity and the owner's triple coming in search of fruit represent one and the same thing. Having thus made a preliminary explanation of today's Gospel, let us pass on to an ordered exposition of all and each one of Christ's words.

"A certain man had a fig tree planted in his vineyard; and he came seeking fruit on it and found none." What can this fig tree mean, if not human nature? And does the woman bowed together not represent the same? It was skillfully planted like the tree, and well nursed, as was the woman; but having fallen, through its own fault, into sin it gives neither fruit of good works nor preserves its uprightness. It fell into sin willfully because it would not bear the fruit of obedience, and thus it lost its uprightness. It did not deign to retain the image of God in which it was rooted and nursed, when it abandoned its original innocence. The owner came three times to the fig tree looking for fruit, because God has loved the human race before the written law, while that law was in force and then when it was fulfilled by the new law of grace, waiting, admonishing and visiting it.

"And he said to the dresser of the vineyard: Behold for these three years I come seeking fruit on this fig tree and I find none." He came before the written law when he gave man, by the light of natural reason, the capacity to judge how he should act towards his neighbor. He came at the time of the written law when he taught men his commandments. He came through grace, after the written law when, of his mercy, he appeared among them. But he complains that he finds the fig tree barren three times in succession, for many perverse minds were neither corrected by the inspired law of nature, nor instructed by his commandments, nor converted by the miracles of his incarnate life. The vine-dresser must represent those who rule the church. The first man to tend the vineyard was Peter; we, however unworthily, follow him in that ministry as often as we labor in your instruction, in teaching, in reproving and in our prayers.

It should inspire us with great fear to hear the master's

words to the vine-dresser: "Cut it down. Why cumbereth it the ground?" Each one of us, as long as we remain on earth, are like the barren fig tree encumbering the ground uselessly, if we fail to produce, each one according to his possibilities, fruits of good works. We are denying others who could take our place more profitably the chance of bearing fruit which we will not bear ourselves. Anyone who enjoys this world's power, if he does not yield a harvest of good actions, is an obstacle to those of other men. Those who are his subjects are incited to wickedness by his iniquitous example, as by the shadow of branches without fruit. Above, the barren tree; below, the barren land: the shadow of the tree is dense, and the foliage permits no ray of sun to reach the ground. So, when a master's life is wicked, his servants, who are his constant witnesses, follow his sterile example, and are deprived of the light of truth. Submerged in his shade they cannot receive the warmth of the sun, because they live estranged from God and are ill-protected in this world. These dissolute potentates are almost forgotten by God: on their road to hell, the only thing he asks them is why they oppress others. So that the master of the vineyard aptly says: "Why cumbereth it the ground?" The ground is unjustly encumbered by the man who tyrannizes the minds of others, by him who will not carry out the good works proper to his position.

Nevertheless, we must pray for such people. For we

hear the vine-dresser's answer: "Lord, let it alone this year also, until I dig about it". What does this digging mean, if not to rebuke those souls which fail to give fruit? As often as we reprove someone for his sins, it is as if we were to dig, as is only right, about a barren tree. Listen, too, to what he means to do after he has dug: "and dung it". What is meant by this dung, if not the remembrance of our sins? In several passages of scripture, the sins of the flesh are referred to as dung. So that God says through his prophet Joel: "The beasts have rotted in their dung" (Joel 1:17). This signifies that those who live carnal lives end their days in the stench of their lust. Therefore, when we reproach such men with their guilt, forcing them to recall and think on their evil actions, it is as if we were to dung a barren tree, so that thus they may be mindful of their wickedness, and obtain the grace of pardon. So the tree is fertilized when we awaken our conscience with the memory of our perverse doings. When the soul is excited by penitence to bewail its former sins, and thus receives the grace to act well, it is as if the root of the heart is manured, rejuvenated, and returns to the fecundity of a good life. Lamenting what it has done, despising what it has been, its intention is set firmly against itself and it is enkindled with desires of amendment. The tree is fertilized back to fruitfulness, as the soul recovers new life through the consideration of its sins. But there are many who listen to the reprimands made them, and nevertheless will not do penance. So they stand green upon this earth, fruitless before God. Hear what the vine-dresser adds: "And if happily it bear fruit; but if not, then after that thou shalt cut it down." He who refuses to be fertilized here by means of our reprehension, in order that he may bear fruit, will be plunged into the next world where penance will no longer be of any avail. He will be cut down then for ever because here he stood green but unfruitful.

The Gospel continues: "And he was teaching in their synagogue on their sabbath. And, behold, there was a woman who had a spirit of infirmity eighteen years..." We have already said that the triple coming of the master of the vineyard in search of fruit, and the eighteen-year disability of this woman signify one and the same thing. In the book of Genesis (Gen. 1:27–31) we read that man was created on the sixth day, and on the same day the work of God was ended. Six multiplied by three makes eighteen. So we see that those eighteen years, during which that woman suffered, represent man's refusal, once he was created on the sixth day, to seek after perfection and his continuance in his weaknesses and sins before the old law was given, during all the time it was in force and after it was perfected by the law of grace, the new law. "And she was bowed together; neither could she look upwards at all." Every sinner heedless of heaven, who thinks only of the earth, is unable to look upwards. Because he pursues earthly desires the rectitude of his mind is bent, and he sees only those things which occupy his thought. Think within you now, brethren, what occupies your thought? One man thinks of honors, another of money, another of his wealth and possessions. All these things are base and vile, and when the mind is busied with them it is deflected from the uprightness of its true dignity. Since it does not aspire to the things of heaven, like the infirm woman, it cannot look upwards.

The Gospel goes on: "Whom when Jesus saw, he called her unto him and said to her: Woman, thou art delivered from thy infirmity. And he laid his hands upon her; and immediately she was made straight." He called her and made her straight, because he helped and enlightened her. He calls us, but he does not straighten us, when we are enlightened by his grace; but it cannot help us because we do not merit help. We often see what we should do, but do not put it into effect; or we attempt it, and give up, discouraged. Our mind sees the upright action, but our strength bows down under it, for it is one of the punishments of sin that by grace we can see what is good conduct, and yet our unworthiness holds us back from its pursuit. Habitual sin fetters the mind so that it is impossible for it to straighten up. It tries to rise but falls back, because it now commits unwillingly those sins which it committed willfully for a long time. The words the psalmist uses of the human race can be applied aptly to this bondage of ours: "I am become miserable, and am bowed down even to the end" (Ps. 37:7). Since man was created to contemplate heavenly light, but, in punishment for his sins, was cast forth into darkness of mind, he now feels no thirst for heaven, tends towards what is mean, desires nothing that endures but turns his mind to earthly things which cripple him and cries within himself saying: "I am become miserable, and am bowed down even to the end." When man was expelled from the contemplation of heavenly things, if he concerned himself only with the necessities of the flesh, he would not have been bowed or brought low in everything. But since not only necessity deprives him of supernatural light, but illicit pleasure also oppresses him heavily, he is not merely bowed, but bowed to the end. So that another prophet rightly says of the evil spirits: "They have said to thy soul: Bow down, that we may go over" (Isa. 51:23). The soul remains upright when it aspires to things of heaven and never stoops to things of the earth. When the wicked spirits see the soul persist in upright actions, they cannot pass over it. They pass over when they bestrew the soul with impure desires. That is why they say: "Bow down that we may go over," because unless the soul itself decides to bow down to earth, their wickedness is powerless against it; they cannot pass over it because they fear its stubborn rectitude.

Let us never, my dear brethren, give entry to those evil spirits by stooping to things of earth and the satisfaction of human appetites. It should cause us shame to stoop to earthly things in this fashion, giving the enemy the chance of passing over us. The man who is bent down looks constantly at the earth; the man who gives his heart to the things of the world forgets the price of his redemption, because he looks for what is vile. Moses rightly prescribed that no hunchback could be raised to the dignity of the priesthood (Lev. 21:20). And all those who have been redeemed by the blood of Jesus Christ have been made members of him, our one High Priest: so God tells us through Peter: "You are a chosen generation, a kingly priesthood" (1 Pet. 2:9). The hunchback goes along with his eyes fixed on the ground: therefore he cannot be a priest, for the man who is intent upon earthly things is witness against himself that he is not a member of this High Priest. We may add that the people of God were forbidden, and rightly so, to eat fish without fins (Lev. 11:10). Fish which have fins and scales usually leap through the water: do they not represent, therefore, the souls of the elect? Beyond any doubt, only those can cross over to the heavenly church who, upheld as it were by the fins of their virtues, leap upwards in their quest for heaven, although they may slip back at times through the weakness of the flesh. Since we discern already, brethren, the happiness of that divine kingdom, let us repent of the time wasted upon worldly matters: let us think of the woman and of the barren fig tree. Mindful of all the evil we have done, let us fertilize our hearts once more, so that when we have enriched and given them new life by penance, they may bear fruit. And even if we cannot practice the highest virtue, God is nevertheless pleased by our desire of repentance. We shall please him merely by beginning those good works which will be a reparation for our wicked actions. Nor shall we lament our sins for long, for very soon eternal joy will wipe those passing tears away. Through our Lord Jesus Christ.

IX.

The Supper

HOMILIA XXXVI IN EVANGELIA

But he said to him: A certain man made a great supper and invited many. And he sent his servant at the hour of supper to say to them that were invited, that they should come; for now all things are ready. And they began all at once to make excuse. The first said to him: I have bought a farm and I must needs go out and see it. I pray thee, hold me excused. And another said: I have bought five yoke of oxen and I go to try them. I pray thee, hold me excused. And another said: I have married a wife; and therefore I cannot come. And the servant, returning, told these things to his lord. Then the master of the house, being angry, said to his servant: Go out quickly into the streets and lanes of the city; and bring in hither the poor and the feeble and the blind and the lame. And the servant said: Lord, it is done as thou hast commanded; and yet there is room. And the Lord said to the servant: Go out into the highways and hedges, and compel them to come in, that my house may be filled. But I say unto you that none of those men that were invited shall taste of my supper. (LUKE 14:16–24)

THERE IS a great difference, dearly beloved brethren, between corporal and spiritual delights in that the former, when we are without them, enkindle in the soul a strong desire to possess them, but once they are attained, they quickly satiate us. Spiritual pleasures, on the contrary, when unattained, produce a certain aversion; but once we taste them, the taste awakens desire, and our hunger for them increases the more we taste them. In the former, desires please us but their realization satiates us: in the latter, the desire is weak but the enjoyment becomes more and more pleasant. In the first, craving is followed by satiety and then aversion: but in the second, appetite is satisfied with a satisfaction which produces desire. For spiritual delights, according as they satisfy us, increase the yearnings of our soul: for the more we taste them the fuller becomes our knowledge of them and the more we love them. So we see that, if we do not taste these delights, we cannot desire them, because their flavor is unknown to us. For who can love what he does not know? So that the psalmist says: "Taste, and see that the Lord is sweet" (Ps. 33:9). As if to say: "You do not know his sweetness, and that is why you do not taste. Open your hearts to the food of life that, tasting its sweetness, you may learn to love it." Man lost these delights when he sinned in paradise: he lost them when he shut his mouth to the everlasting food. So that we, born in the distress of this our pilgrimage, come to the world already squeamish. We do not know what we should desire, and our repugnance is increased the further our souls stray from that true nourishment. It does not seek interior delights, because it has long lost the habit of tasting them. So we waste away and our loathing wears us out by the long abstinence it imposes on us. God's mercy, however, does not abandon us even when we abandon him.

For he recalls to our memory those spiritual joys, and offers them to us: he shakes our sloth with generous promises and entices us to cast off this nausea. For he tells us: "A certain man made a great supper and invited many." Is this not the man of whom the prophet speaks when he says: "And he is a man, and who has known him?" (Jer. 17:9†), who prepared a great supper when he prepared for us a feast of everlasting relish? This man called many and few came: because sometimes those who are his subjects by faith, turn their backs upon that heavenly banquet by the wickedness of their lives.

The Gospel continues: "And he sent his servant at the hour of supper to say to them that were invited, that they should come." The hour of the supper is the end of the world, which the apostle Paul tells us is very near: "We... upon whom the ends of the world are come" (1 Cor. 10:2).

---

†   The best Latin texts here give: *Pravum est cor omnium, et inscrutabile: quis cognoscet illud?* and not: *Et homo est, et quis cognovit eum*—as quoted by St. Gregory. (TRANSLATOR)

Since we see, then, that we are called at the very hour of supper, that is, when the world is nearing its end, we must not excuse ourselves from attending God's banquet. Since we believe also that everything in this world is merely transitory, let us take care that this time of grace should not pass to no avail. This feast to which God invites us is called supper and not dinner, because supper is the last meal of the day. Since God's eternal banquet is our consummation, it is rightly compared to that final meal. Furthermore, we must see that the servant sent with invitations by the master of the household represents the preachers of the church. Being one of them, although unworthy and oppressed by the weight of my sins, nevertheless when I speak for your instruction, I also am a servant of that master. When I exhort you to despise this world, I come to invite you to God's feast. Let no one despise me, then, for my personal defects: for although I am unworthy, the joys I promise are immense. It often happens, brethren, that a powerful person has a contemptible servant, and when he sends a message by him, to relations or to strangers, the person of the servant is not despised, for the sake of the master who sent him. Those who hear him do not think of the person who speaks, but only of the message he brings and the person whose message it is. So you, brethren, must do the same; and if perhaps you consider us preachers unworthy, nevertheless venerate God who calls you through us. Be willing

guests at the table of the master of the house. Rid yourselves of that fatal lack of appetite, for all things are prepared to cure you of it. But if you are still carnally-minded,
it may be that you look for carnal feasts. Do you not recall
that flesh, for your sake, has become spiritual nourishment?
To rid our heart of that aversion, the Lamb was immolated
for you at the Lord's supper.

But what do we do when we see so many act as those of
whom the Gospel says: "And they began all at once to make
excuse"? God offers freely what should be implored of him;
he wishes to give unasked that for which we should scarcely
dare to hope, and his offer is despised. He tells them that
the delights of the everlasting feast are now ready, and yet
they all at once begin to make excuse. Let us consider a lesser example, so that we may fully understand the lesson. If a
rich and powerful man were to invite a poor one to dine, I
ask you brethren, what would the latter do? Would he not
rejoice at the very honor of the invitation, accepting with
humility? Would he not change his clothes, and hurry to
see to it that he should be the first at the feast? When a rich
man sends an invitation, the poor man loses no time in pre-
senting himself: but we seek excuses, when it is God who
invites us. But already I foresee what you answer in your
inmost thoughts, in your hearts: "We do not seek excuses.
We are very glad to be called, and to be there at the eternal
supper."

Your heart speaks the truth, if it is true that you do not prefer the things of earth to those of heaven: provided that you long for the riches of heaven, and not those of earth. The Gospel tells us the reason why each guest wishes to be excused: "The first said to him: I have bought a farm and I must needs go out and see it. I pray thee, hold me excused." Does not the farm signify worldly possessions? That man goes to see his farm, who thinks only of material things and the wealth they bring him. "And another said: I have bought five yoke of oxen and I go to try them. I pray thee, hold me excused." What are we to understand by the five oxen, if not the five senses of the body? Indeed rightly are they called a yoke, because they go in pairs, in both sexes. The corporal senses, unable to understand spiritual things, knowing only what is material and external, devote themselves to what is tangible: they can be taken as a symbol of curiosity. For the senses, while they wish to know of other people's lives, know nothing of the soul. The vice of curiosity is a dangerous one, for it inclines its victim to discover the conduct of his neighbor, while he is ignorant of his own inner self; so that, knowing others' business, he will not know his own; and examining another's virtues he will ignore the measure of his own. That is why we are told the man replied: "I go to try them. I pray thee, hold me excused." It is noteworthy that the very words of his excuse reveal the vice which has taken control of him, because he says: "I go to try them." Sometimes a trial is merely to satisfy curiosity. But we should notice that the man who excuses himself because of the farm he has bought, as well as the man who uses his oxen as an excuse, does so in words of humility; both say: "I pray thee, hold me excused." But when they say: "I pray thee," and at the same time refuse to assist, they show humility in their speech but pride in their actions. Notice that every wicked man condemns this course of action when it is pointed out to him: nevertheless he does no otherwise himself. When we say to a sinner: "Repent; seek only God; leave this world," do we not invite him to God's banquet? But when he answers "Pray for me because I am a sinner, and unable to do as you say," does he not seek indulgence at the same time as he makes excuse? With these words: I am a sinner, he makes a show of humility, but on adding: I cannot repent, he shows obvious pride. He, then, uses a prayer as an excuse, whose words are humble but whose actions are proud.

And another said: "I have married a wife; and therefore I cannot come." Does not the wife in this parable signify the pleasures of the flesh? For although matrimony is good and has been instituted by God for the propagation of the race, there are some who desire it, not for this end, but for the satisfaction of their own passions; and therefore there is nothing objectionable in representing something illicit by something quite licit. The great Father of all, then, invites you to the supper of eternal life: but, one is given over to avarice, another to curiosity, another to the pleasures of the flesh: unanimously they make their excuse. While one busies himself with worldly dealings, another racks his brain with the concerns of others and the third smears his mind with carnal pleasures: none makes any effort to hurry to the banquet of everlasting bliss.

"And the servant, returning, told these things to his lord. Then the master of the house, being angry, said to his servant: Go out quickly into the streets and lanes of the city; and bring in hither the poor and the feeble and the blind and the lame." Thus he who devotes himself excessively to earthly matters refuses to attend; he who enquires curiously into his neighbor's life has no hunger for that spiritual nourishment; he who surrenders himself to the lusts of the flesh rejects the delicacies of the spiritual banquet. Since, then, the proud refuse to come, the poor are chosen. And why is this? Because, as Paul tells us: "The weak things of the world hath God chosen, that he may confound the strong" (1 Cor. 1:27). We should note the description of those who are summoned to the feast and who attend: "the poor and the feeble." They are called poor and feeble who, according to their own estimation, are weak. For those who are proud in their poverty are truly poor although they may appear strong. They are blind who lack the light of understanding; they are lame who are not upright in their actions. But while these vices of character can be represented by infirmities of the limbs, it is apparent that just as those who refused to attend when called were sinners, so also are they sinners who are called and who do, in fact, attend. But the proud sinners are rejected while the humble are chosen.

God chooses those whom the world despises, because it often happens that the very contempt of which they are the object brings self-knowledge. Thus he who left his father and home and wasted the inheritance he had received, did not come to his senses until he felt the pangs of hunger, and thought: "How many hired servants in my father's house abound with bread" (Luke 15:17). He had wandered far from self-knowledge when he sinned, and if he had not experienced such misery, he would never have attained it. Only when he was in need of temporal goods did he think of spiritual goods. Thus the poor, the feeble, the blind and the lame are called and they attend, for the weak and those whom this world despises hear God's voice more swiftly because they find nothing to delight them in this world. All this is well signified in that young Egyptian, servant of the Amalecite (1 Kgs. 30ff.), who, while they made their raids and robberies, lay sick upon the roadside, starved and parched with thirst. When David found him he gave him food and drink, so that when his health returned he became David's guide. Surprising the Amalecites at their feasting, this young Egyptian helped to overthrow those who had abandoned him when he was ill. The Amalecites are called a licking race. What can this indicate if not the condition of the worldly minded? For it is as if they licked those worldly things which are the sole satisfaction of their ambition. And, like the Amalecites, they too are robbers: desirous of earthly good which they heap up at others' expense. But, like the young Egyptian whom his master abandoned sick on the road, every sinner, once he grows sick in worldly prosperity, soon earns the contempt of the worldly minded. But when David found the youth, he gave him food and drink, because God who is strong does not despise those whom the world rejects. He often converts them to grace and to his love. He gives the food and drink of his divine word to those who fail to keep up with the world and remain, as it were, by the wayside. He chooses them as his guides in this life, and makes them his preachers. When they bring Christ to the heart of sinners, they lead David, as it were, to the conquest of his enemies. With him they strike the feasting Amalecites off guard: because by the grace of God they bring low those proud men who in this world had despised them. The young Egyptian slays the Amalecites: because often those preachers sway the outlook of the worldly minded with whom they could not keep pace before in the race for worldly honour.

But let us hear the servant's words now that he has

led the poor into the feast: "Lord it is done as thou hast commanded; and yet there is room." Many of the Jews were gathered for the Lord's supper, but the numbers of that people which believed in Jesus Christ did not fill the hall of the eternal supper. Many Jews entered but still there was room left in the kingdom to be filled by many of the Gentiles.

So the lord says to his servant: "Go out into the highways and hedges, and compel them to come in, that my house may be filled." When our Lord invites to his feast those whom his servants find in the streets and lanes of the city, he is referring to people who kept his law while going about their business in the cities: but when he orders them to be called from the highways and the hedges, he is indicating a rustic people, that is, the Gentiles. This is how we understand the psalmist's phrase: "then shall all the trees of the woods rejoice before the face of the Lord, because he cometh" (Ps. 95:13). The Gentiles were called the trees of the wood because in their infidelity they were always twisted and without fruit. So that those who were converted from that rustic state came to the eternal supper as if from the hedges.

We should notice too that, in this third invitation, the servant is not told to invite, but to compel. Some are called and will not come; others are called and come; finally, there are others of whom we may say that they are not called, but compelled, to come. Those are called but refuse to come, who receive the gift of understanding, but fail to act according to its dictates. Those are called and come, who by their good works perfect the intellectual grace which they receive. There are some who are called in such a way that they have no option, but to attend: as there are some who understand perfectly the good they should do, but do not do it; they see the proper course of action, but they do not want to follow it. As we said before, it is most frequently these men who are forestalled in their temporal ambitions by the adversities of this world. They seek earthly glory and fail to achieve it, and while they try to navigate the high seas in pursuit of important affairs, they are continually driven back by contrary currents towards the shores of humiliation. Seeing themselves thwarted in all their desires, then they remember all they owe to their Maker: very much ashamed, they return to him whom, in the blindness of their vanity, they had once abandoned. We see also that some, who are anxious to attain the summit of temporal success, either fall victims to a long illness, or are afflicted with serious trials. Worn out by serious injuries, this world's pain teaches them not to trust in its delights and, rebuking themselves for their former yearnings, they turn their heart to the Lord. God, indeed, has said of them through his prophet: "I will hedge up thy way with thorns and I will stop it up with a wall: and she shall not find her paths. And she shall follow after her lovers and shall not overtake them: and she shall seek them and shall not find. And she shall say: I will go and return to my first husband, because it was better with me then, than now" (Hos. 2:6–7). The husband of every faithful soul is God, because it is united with him by faith. But the soul "shall follow after her lovers" when it professes its belief in God, yet, by its deeds, prostrates itself before unclean spirits, seeking this world's glory: when it enjoys carnal pleasures and feeds on voluptuous delights. But God often takes pity on such a soul, and mingles bitterness with its satisfactions. So, it is said: "I will hedge up thy way with thorns." Our way is hedged with thorns when we feel the painful pricking of sadness in that very thing we wickedly desired. "And I will stop it up with a wall: and she shall not find her paths." Our ways are blocked when serious difficulties oppose our earthly ambitions; we cannot find our paths because we are prevented from attaining our evil desires. "And she shall follow after her lovers and shall not overtake them," as the soul cannot reach those unclean spirits to which, in order to achieve her ends, she subjected herself. However, the usefulness and the spiritual advantage which result from this adversity are seen when the passage continues: "And she shall say: I will go and return to my first husband, because it was better with me then, than now." When she finds her way hedged in with thorns, when she fails to find her lovers, then she returns to the love of her first husband: as often, when we cannot obtain what we desire, when we are exhausted by the impossibility of realizing our earthly wishes, we turn our mind to God. What displeased us formerly, now gives us pleasure; suddenly he, whose precepts were so bitter to us once, becomes sweet to contemplate; and the soul, which had tried to be an adulteress but had failed because of external obstacles, determines to be faithful. Can we not say, then, that those who, wounded by this world's afflictions, return to the love of God and renounce their vices, are compelled, so to speak, to enter?

Truly terrible is the condemnation uttered by our Lord against those who were called and would not come. Listen to it attentively, brethren and masters: brethren those who are sinners, and masters those who are just. Try to listen carefully so that, by feeling more fear here, you may feel less at the judgment. He says: "I say unto you that none of those men that were invited shall taste of my supper." See how he invites through himself, through his angels, through the patriarchs, the prophets, the apostles and the pastors of the church, and he invites also through us. He invites sometimes through miracles, again through punishments; sometimes through worldly prosperity and again through adversities. If anyone despises this summons, if anyone excuses himself when he is invited, he may not be allowed to enter when he knocks. Hear what Wisdom says through Solomon: "Then shall they call upon me, and I will not hear: they shall rise in the morning and shall not find me" (Proverbs 1:28). This is why the foolish virgins, coming late, cry out and say: "Lord, Lord, open to us." But the answer given to those who wish to enter is: "Amen, I say to you, I know you not" (Matt. 25:11–12). With this terrible sentence before our eyes, must we not abandon all the things of this world, make little of its worries and aspire to heaven only? But this is a privilege which is granted only to few.

I desire, but I do not dare, to advise you to leave all earthly goods. But, if you cannot abandon everything, at least possess what you have in such a way that you are free of it: so that your temporal wealth is possessed, and does not possess you. Preserve your mastery over it, rather than allow your heart to be swayed and dominated by things of lesser value than itself. Let these earthly things be of use to us, while our desires speed towards what is eternal. The former are of value while we are on our way, but we desire the latter at our journey's end. So we should regard with detachment, as it were with indifference, all that happens in this world. The eyes of the soul must look straight ahead, fixed upon the end of our journey. Our vices, once uprooted, must find soil no longer, either in our actions or in our hearts. Neither the pleasures of the flesh, nor curiosity, nor the heat of ambition must ever be allowed to impede our entry to that supper of the Lord. We must treat with a holy indifference, even our good actions here, so that those earthly things which please the body can in no way harm the soul. I do not dare to tell you to leave all you possess; but if you really are desirous of doing so, you can leave it at the same time as you retain it: that is, if you so administer your temporal riches that your soul is wholly bent on those which last for ever.

So the apostle Paul tells us: "The time is short. It remaineth that they also who have wives be as if they had none; and they that weep, as though they wept not; and they that rejoice, as if they rejoiced not; and they that buy, as though they possessed not; and they that use this world, as if they used it not. For the fashion of this world passeth away" (1 Cor. 7:29ff.). He has a wife as if he had none who can pay the marriage debt in such fashion as to preserve himself from bondage to this world's pleasure. Elsewhere the same illustrious teacher tells us: "He that is with a wife is solicitous for the things of the world; how he may please his wife" (1 Cor. 7:33). It is evident that the man, who seeks to please his wife in a way which does not displease his Maker, has indeed a wife, but is as if he had none. He weeps, but as if he did not weep, who is afflicted by temporal loss, but whose soul finds consolation in the thought of eternal gain. That man rejoices, but as if he did not, who so enjoys earthly benefits as never to forget the eternal torments, always moderating the exaltation of his spirits with a salutary fear.

He buys as if he did not possess, who provides himself with all outward necessaries, but does not forget that soon he must leave them behind him. He uses this world as if he had no use for it, who provides himself with what is necessary to live, but nevertheless does not allow those things to conquer his heart; so that what is of service to him externally does not deflect the course of his soul which aspires to higher things. Those who act in this way do not possess things merely to satisfy their desires, but rather to put them to use; they use whatever they need, but they have no sinful avarice. And even through those very possessions, they are rewarded, for they take greater pleasure in works of mercy than in their store of wealth.

Lest this seem difficult to some of you, I am going to tell you an incident which concerns a certain person known to many of you. I have the witness of trustworthy inhabitants of the city of Civitavechia that this really happened, about three years ago. About this time Count Theophanius lived there: a man devoted to deeds of kindness, and hospitable above measure. Busied with the affairs of his estates, he dealt with temporal and mundane matters: it became known after his death that this was more from a sense of duty than from preference. When he was dying, a dreadful storm made it clear that it would be impossible to carry him to the sepulcher. His wife, in tears, complained: "What shall I do? How can I bring you to burial, when this tempest prevents me from crossing the threshold?" The-ophanius replied: "Do not weep, woman, for as soon as I am dead, the tempest will be stilled." As soon as he had said this he died, and at the same moment there was a lull in the storm. His hands and feet were swollen and ulcerated by gout, and were issuing pus. But, when they uncovered the body to wash it, as is the custom, his hands and feet were seen to be as clean as if they had never known a trace of any wound. Four days after burial, his wife thought it bet-ter to change the marble slab which had been placed over the tomb. When it was removed, such a fragrance came from his body as if, from that putrefying flesh, there issued heavenly perfumes instead of worms. I have told you this, so that you may see from such a recent example that there are people in secular and worldly dress, who have not a worldly mind. Those who find that necessity obliges them to remain in the world, so that they cannot leave it alto-gether, should so esteem those worldly matters as not to subject their minds to them. Meditate on this, and since you cannot abandon them, fulfill your exterior obligations as best you can, while inwardly you hasten towards that which lasts for ever. Nothing should delay this desire of your soul: let no delight of this world enmesh you. If you love good, love what is better, that is, what is of heaven. If you fear evil, reflect upon everlasting evils, so that, looking at what is most to be loved and what is most to be feared, we may not be attached to things present. In order to do this, we have the mediator between God and men, through whom we shall obtain all things if we burn with ardent love for him who lives and reigns with the Father and the Holy Ghost, God for ever and ever. Amen.

X.

The Lost Sheep and the Lost Coin

HOMILIA XXXIV IN EVANGELIA

Now the publicans and sinners drew near unto him to hear him. And the Pharisees and the scribes murmured, saying: This man receiveth sinners and eateth with them. And he spoke to them this parable, saying: What man of you that hath an hundred sheep, and if he shall lose one of them, doth he not leave the ninety-nine in the desert and go after that which was lost, until he find it? And, when he hath found it, lay it upon his shoulders, rejoicing? And, coming home, call together his friends and neighbors, saying to them: Rejoice with me, because I have found my sheep that was lost? I say to you that even so there shall be joy in heaven upon one sinner that doth penance, more than upon ninety-nine just who need not penance. Or, what woman having ten coins, if she lose one coin, doth not light a candle and sweep the house and seek diligently until she find it? And, when she hath found it, call together her friends and neighbors, saying: Rejoice with me, because I have found the coin which I had lost. So I say to you, there shall be

joy before the angels of God upon one sinner doing penance.
(LUKE 15:1–10)

YOU HAVE seen, dearly beloved, in reading this Gospel, that the publicans and the sinners approached our Redeemer and were received, not only to converse, but also to eat with him. And the pharisees, seeing it, were indignant. From this fact, we can deduce that true justice feels pity, while that which is false feels indignation, although it does sometimes happen that the just rightly feel anger against sinners. But action prompted by pride is one thing, while that which springs from zeal for good is quite another. Those who have this zeal are indignant, but not enraged: they despair, but are not without hope: they instigate reprisals, but through love, for although outwardly they seem to exaggerate their rebukes and corrections, inwardly they conserve that mildness which is the fruit of charity. In their hearts they have a greater love for those whom they reprove than for themselves: they consider those whom they discipline as their betters. By this course of action, they keep their subjects in order, and themselves in humility. On the contrary, those who are motivated by a false sense of justice, usually despise others and have no pity for the weak. Through their presumption in thinking themselves sinless, they sink lower than those whom they disdain. The pharisees were men of this type: they judged Christ because he received sinners; in their sterile hearts, they rebuked the very Fount of all mercy.

Since these sinners were sick people who were unaware of their illness because they did not know themselves, the heavenly physician sought pleasant remedies to cure them. In order to arrest that tumor in their heart, he propounded for their consideration a moving comparison. So he says: "What man of you that hath an hundred sheep, and if he shall lose one of them, doth he not leave the ninety-nine in the desert and go after that which was lost, until he find it?" Notice the wonderful example of mercy which Jesus gives in this parable, mercy which man might find in himself, yet which belongs in a particular manner to the Creator of men. As one hundred is a perfect number, God had one hundred sheep when he created angels and men. But one sheep was lost: for man sinned and abandoned the pastures of life. But their shepherd left the ninety-nine in the desert: he left all those lofty choirs of angels in heaven. How can heaven be called a desert, unless it is because it was deserted? Man deserted it when he sinned, but the ninety-nine sheep remained in the desert while God went to seek the straying one here on earth. The number of rational creatures, that is of angels and men, which had been created to see God, was diminished when man fell: and so that the perfect number of sheep might be maintained in heaven, God followed the lost human race down to earth.

But where Luke tells us, "in the desert," Matthew, in the same context, says: "in the mountains," as if to indicate that the ninety-nine which did not stray remained in the heights, that is, in heaven. "And, when he hath found it, lay it upon his shoulders, rejoicing." He put the sheep upon his shoulders because, taking on himself our human nature, he bore our sins. "And, coming home, call together his friends and neighbors, saying to them: Rejoice with me, because I have found my sheep that was lost." When he has found the sheep he returns home: because our shepherd returned to heaven, once man had been redeemed. There he finds his friends and neighbors, the choirs of angels. They are his true friends, whose constancy in carrying out his will has never wavered. They are his neighbors, moreover, because they enjoy clear vision of him by their unceasing attendance. It is noteworthy that he does not say: "Rejoice with the sheep restored," but, "Rejoice with me," because his joy is our life and when we are restored to heaven, the fullness of his joy will be achieved.

"I say to you that even so there shall be joy in heaven upon one sinner that doth penance, more than upon ninety-nine just who need not penance." We must consider, brethren, why our Lord says that there is more joy in heaven for converted sinners than for the perseverance of the just. Is it not our common experience that many who do not have to bear the weight of sin upon their conscience, who tread the path of justice and are strangers to the illicit, nevertheless do not feel any great anxiety to reach their heavenly home? They allow themselves the use of what is lawful all the more freely since they know they have done nothing unlawful. Very often they are slow to practice the most important virtues, because they are sure of never having committed a grave sin. Sometimes, on the other hand, those who are conscious of having committed sin are touched by their own remorse, and, enkindled with the love of God, they practice the greatest virtues. They face all difficulties with a most holy courage; they abandon all worldly things; they flee all honors; they rejoice in the contempt they receive from others; they are on fire with heavenly desires and a longing to attain their everlasting home; realizing that they have strayed from God so far, they make up for their former offences by the profit they earn later. There is more joy, then, in heaven for the return of a sinner than for the constancy of the just man; as in a battle the captain will prefer the soldier who, having fled, returns to attack the enemy more courageously, to him who never ran away, but who never performs a deed of valour. So also the laborer esteems more highly that ground which once produced only thorns and now brings forth rich fruit, than that which has no thorns but which does not give a fertile harvest.

In spite of all this it cannot be denied that in the lives of some just men there is cause for joy such as cannot be counted as less than that felt upon a sinner's return. There are many who know that they are not guilty of any sin, and yet they mortify themselves as if guilty of all the sins in the world. They reject all comforts, even what is lawful; they welcome the scorn of others; they will not allow themselves the least pleasure but abstain from enjoying even those things which have been permitted them; they despise material things and are enkindled with desire for what is unseen; they find their joy in suffering and humble themselves in everything; and as some weep for their sins of action, they bewail the sins of thought. How can I describe them? Just penitents, who humble themselves in penance for sins of thought and always remain upright in their actions. So we can imagine God's joy on seeing the humble tears of the just man, when there is such rejoicing in heaven for the sinner who makes good, by penance, the evil he committed.

The Gospel continues: "Or, what woman having ten coins, if she lose one coin, doth not light a candle and sweep the house and seek diligently until she find it?" This woman and the shepherd have a common significance: for they both stand for God and God's wisdom. Since the coin is a coin which bears an image, the woman lost the coin when man, created in the image of God, strayed by sin from this resemblance to his Maker. But the woman lights her lamp, for the wisdom of God appeared among men. A lamp is simply a light placed upon a stand, but here the light is the divinity made man. And he who is Wisdom, in the words of the psalm, says of the lampstand of his body: "My strength is dried up like a potsherd" (Ps. 21:16). For, as the clay is hardened by fire, his strength is dried up like that clay; that is to say, that by the sufferings of his passion he fortified the flesh he had assumed for the glory of the resurrection. The lamp once lit, however, the house is ransacked, for as soon as his divinity appeared in the flesh, the conscience of man was upset by the realization of its great guilt. The word *evertere* which means to overturn is not dissimilar to the word *emundare* meaning to sweep, for if the degraded intelligence is not overturned first by fear, it will never be cleansed of its habitual vices. When the house has been ransacked the coin is discovered, because when man's conscience is disturbed, he recovers the image of his Maker. "And, when she hath found it, call together her friends and neighbors, saying: Rejoice with me, because I have found the coin which I had lost." Who are those friends and neighbors, if not those heavenly powers of whom we spoke before? These are always near the divine wisdom because the grace of its continual presence enlightens them. But, thinking of these things, let us not forget the reason why this woman, who represents God's wisdom, is said to have had ten coins, of which she loses one and finds it again after a search. God made angels and men in order to know him, and in giving them eternal life, undoubtedly he formed

ST. GREGORY THE GREAT

them to his image. The woman had ten coins: because there are nine choirs of angels. But so that the number of the elect might be complete, man was created. He was not lost to his Creator even after his transgression, because God's eternal wisdom, shining for all to see in the miracles he performed on earth, repaired that sin by the light of his bodily presence, as a lamp on a lampstand.

We have said that there is a ninefold order of angels, because from Holy Scripture we know that there are angels, archangels, virtues, powers, principalities, dominations, thrones, cherubim and seraphim. Almost all the pages of Scripture attest that there are angels and archangels. We all know that the books of the prophets speak of cherubim and seraphim. And the apostle Paul, writing to the Ephesians, quotes the names of four ranks of them: "Above all principality and power and virtue and dominion" (Eph. 1:21); and writing to the Colossians he declares: "Whether thrones, or dominations, or principalities, or powers" (Col. 1:16). When he wrote to the Ephesians he names the powers, dominations and principalities, but speaking to the Colossians in the same context he adds the thrones, of which he said nothing to the Ephesians. When we add these latter, we have five orders which are indicated in a special way in Holy Scripture. Adding these five to the angels, archangels, cherubim and seraphim, we find nine choirs of angels. So that the prophet says to the first angel created: "Thou wast the seal of resemblance, full of wisdom and perfect in beauty. Thou wast in the pleasures of the paradise of God" (Ezech. 28:12–13). We should note in this passage that he is not said to be made merely in the likeness of God, but the very seal of that likeness, to show that, as his nature is more subtle, the resemblance is more complete. And the same prophet adds: "Every precious stone was thy covering: the sardius, the topaz and the jasper, the chrysolite and the onyx and the beryl, the sapphire and the carbuncle and the emerald." Notice that nine classes of stones are cited, as there are nine orders of angels. That first angel was adorned and beautified with the nine orders as he was esteemed above all the other angels: uniting all their virtues in one, he outshone the rest.

But now that we have stopped to consider the angelic orders which exist, should we not mention the different functions of each? In Greek the angels are called "messengers," and the archangels "supreme messengers." We know that this name refers to their office, not to their nature. In that divine fatherland the holy spirits are indeed always spirits, but they cannot be called angels always, since they are such only when through them something is announced. So the psalmist says: "Who makest thy angels spirits" (Ps. 103:4), as if to say: "Who, when he wishes, makes angels of those who serve him as spirits." Those who bring messages of less moment are called angels; those who bring the more important are called archangels. That is why not just any angel, but the archangel Gabriel was deputed to bring tidings to our Lady; for it seemed fitting to send a higher angel to carry out that important duty of heralding the greatest of all good news. The angels are also given specific names, to show by them what is the particular work of each. In that supreme city illumined with all the knowledge which comes from the vision of God, they do not need names in order to be distinguished from each other; but when they come to discharge some function among us, they take the name of the function itself.

So, Michael means: "who is like unto God"; Gabriel, "strength of God," and Raphael, "medicine of God." And whenever some deed is wrought of extraordinary strength, we say that Michael has been sent, to show that, in that action and by the use of that name, no one can do as much as almighty God. So the ancient enemy who, incited by pride and wishing to make himself like unto God, said: "I will ascend into heaven. I will exalt my throne above the stars of God. I will sit in the mountain of the covenant, in the sides of the north. I will ascend above the height of the clouds. I will be like the most High" (Isa. 14:13–14), while at the end of the world he will be left to linger in his eternal torment, is represented as having battled with the archangel Michael. As we are told by John: "There was a great battle in heaven. Michael and his angels fought with the dragon" (Rev. 12:7). Thus he who proudly thought himself like to God should learn from his defeat by Michael that no one becomes like God through pride. Mary was visited by the archangel Gabriel, who is called the strength of God. He came to herald him who deigned to appear in great lowliness in order to subdue the wicked angels. Of him the psalmist says: "Lift up your gates, O ye princes, and be ye lifted up, O eternal gates: and the King of Glory shall enter in. Who is this King of Glory? The Lord who is strong and mighty: the Lord mighty in battle" (Ps. 23:7–10). And in the same place he says: "The Lord of hosts, he is the King of Glory." Then it was proper that the Lord of hosts, strong and mighty in the battle he had come to wage upon the wicked angels, should be heralded by the "strength of God." Raphael's name, as we said, means medicine of God; and we see that he cured the blindness of Tobias by touching his eyes. He who was sent to heal is rightly called the medicine of God. We have touched on the interpretation of the angels' names; it remains now to deal briefly with their offices.

Those spirits are called virtues by whose agency signs and miracles are most frequently performed. Those are called powers whose order has received more power than the others, so that the malignant spirits are subject to their dominion, and are restrained by them from tempting man as far as otherwise they would. The principalities are those who preside over the good angels, and give them orders when something has to be done in fulfillment of the divine service. Dominations are those which are superior to the principalities; for to be a prince is to be the first among others: but to dominate is to have others as one's subjects. That is why those heavenly hosts which surpass the others in strength, in that the others owe them obedience, are called dominations. The thrones are those celestial hosts presided over by God when he executes his judgments. In Latin the thrones are called seats, and those spirits are called thrones of God which so abound in divine grace as if God rested on them to carry out his judgments by means of them. So the psalmist says: "Thou hast sat on the throne who judgest justice" (Ps. 9:5). The cherubim are also called the fullness of knowledge. Those sublime hosts are called cherubim because they enjoy a perfection of knowledge in proportion to their nearness to the brightness of God. As far as creatures can, they know all things, because, by the merit of their rank, they see God most clearly. The seraphim are those heavenly hosts which, by reason of their closeness to God, burn with an extraordinary love for him. Seraphim means burning, or enkindled. These, because they are so near God, for no other spirit exists between him and them, are fired all the more to love him by that proximity. Love is the flame which animates them, for seeing that unsullied splendor so closely, their love burns most ardently.

But of what use is it to dwell upon the gifts and graces with which the angels are blessed unless, by apt reflection, we draw some profit to ourselves? That heavenly city is inhabited by angels and men. There, as we believe, will enter only those numbers of the human race which equal those of the angels who remained faithful to God. For it is written: "He appointed the bounds of people according to the number of the angels of God" (Deut. 32:8[†]). Therefore we must say something of the distinctions which exist between the different citizens of heaven, hoping that we ourselves may increase in virtue by these reflections. We believe that the number of men who are to reach heaven will be equivalent to that of the angels who remained loyal to God. Therefore it is necessary that those men who advance towards their heavenly home should imitate upon the way, to some extent at least, the virtues of their fellow-citizens. For the different occupations of men resemble those of the different angelic orders, and each man is allotted to his class by that characteristic similarity of occupation. There are many who have only little capacity for understanding; nevertheless, they use what they have well, so that their brothers profit by their teaching. These will be classed among the angels.

[†]   The best Latin texts here give: *Constituit terminos populorum juxta numerum filiorum Israel*, and not: *Statuit terminos gentium secundum numerum angelorum Dei*—as quoted by St. Gregory. (TRANSLATOR)

There are others who, aided by divine grace, understand and expound the most supreme mysteries of God, and to these we must assign a place among the archangels. There are others who have the gift of working miracles and performing marvelous deeds: where are these to be set, if not among the virtues? There are some who can make the evil spirits flee in terror, who banish them from the bodies they possess, by virtue of their prayers and the heavenly power they enjoy. Having regard to their great merit, must we not consider these people as kindred to the heavenly powers? There are a few who, by the virtues which they received, transcend the worth even of the elect: since they are better than the good, they preside over their brothers in justice. What will be their lot, if not a place among the principalities? And yet others are in such control of themselves, in their vices and their desires that for their purity of life they are called gods among men; so it was said to Moses: "I have appointed thee the God of Pharao" (Exod. 7:1). These are surely numbered among the dominations. Some who, by watchful care, dominate themselves and solicitously examine the rectitude of their intention and cleave constantly to a filial fear of God, receive, as a reward for their virtue, the capacity of clear-headed judgment of others. As their mind is clarified by the divine contemplation, God presides there as from his throne, and judges others' actions and enacts his will through them. These are the thrones of their Maker;

they guide and rule his church, and often judge even the elect for their faults of weakness. So also there are many people who are so filled with love for God and for their neighbor, that truly they may be classed as cherubim. As we have said, cherubim means fullness of knowledge, and from St. Paul we learn that: "Love is the fulfilling of the law" (Romans 13:10). Therefore those who have greater love of God and of their neighbor than have others, are worthy to be ranked among the cherubim. Lastly come those who burn with the fire of supernatural contemplation. Seeking only union with their Maker, they no longer look for anything of this earth; loving only the things of eternity, they despise all that is worldly. Their thoughts rise above all temporal goods, they love and are inflamed with love, finding rest among those flames. Alight with love, their speech sets fire to others: those to whom they speak soon feel the ardor of God's love. What shall I call them, if not seraphim? Their heart becomes a fire and gives light and heat, for it enlightens the eyes of the understanding to supernatural things, inspiring it with tears of compunction, which clean the soul of all its vices. Is it not among the seraphim that those who are so inflamed with love of God reach their destiny?

As I speak to you of these things, dearly beloved, recollect yourselves, and examine your merits inwardly. See whether your good actions are sincere; see whether you find the fulfillment of your present conduct among those hosts of angels of whom I have spoken, although briefly. Unhappy is that soul which cannot find in itself any of those virtues which we have mentioned. But more pitiable still is its state if it sees itself lacking in them and does not weep. The man who reacts in this fashion, brethren, is to be pitied, because he does not pity himself. Let us think, then, of these gifts and graces which adorn the just, and put all our energies into the attainment of such good fortune. Let him bewail himself who finds no grace within him. But the man who finds in himself some virtue, however slight it may be, must not covet the great virtues with which others abound; for those supreme ranks of angels are so created that some are given pre-eminence over others. It is told that St. Dionysius the Areopagite, an ancient and venerable father, used to say that, for the discharge of any office one or more of the inferior angels were sent, either visibly or invisibly; for in order to console man angels or archangels are sent from heaven. The higher ranks never leave the inner sanctum, for those which are more excellent are not employed in outward tasks. This seems to contradict the words of Isaias, who says: "And one of the seraphims flew to me: and in his hand was a live coal, which he had taken with the tongs off the altar. And he touched my mouth" (Isa. 6:6–7). But when reading this passage of the prophet, it must be understood that those spirits which are sent receive their name from the office they fulfill. So the angel who burns away the sins of the tongue carries a coal from the altar and is called seraphim, as that word means fire. This is the sense we should give to Daniel's words: "Thousands of thousands ministered to him, and ten thousand times a hundred thousand stood before him" (Dan. 7:10). It is one thing to minister, and another to stand in his presence. Those minister to God who leave heaven as his messengers but those stand before him who so enjoy the intimate vision of him that they are sent very seldom upon any outside mission.

But although we learn from certain passages of Scripture that the function of the cherubim differs from that of the seraphim, for lack of conclusive proof, we do not wish to affirm whether they perform their office themselves or discharge it through other angels, as has been affirmed. However, we do know with certainty that some spirits command others to fulfill the divine wishes. The prophet Zacharias testifies to this when he says: "And, behold, the angel that spoke in me went forth: and another angel went out to meet him. And he said to him: Run, speak to this young man, saying: Jerusalem shall be inhabited without walls" (Zach. 2:3–4). When one angel says to another: "Run and speak," it is clear that one commands the other; and if that is so, then some angels are superior to others. And with regard to those angels who are sent to us, we are sure that, while they come in the performance of an outward service, they do not fail to discharge their inward office of contemplation.

So they are sent and at the same time they stand in the presence of God, because, although the angelic spirit is limited, the supreme spirit, God himself, is infinite. The angels, then, are sent, yet stand in his presence: because no matter where they go, they continue to move in him.

It is noteworthy, too, that the angels are frequently given the name of the order or group which follows. We said that the thrones, that is, the seats of God, form a special order of blessed spirits; nevertheless, the psalmist says: "Thou that sittest upon the cherubims; shine forth" (Ps. 79:2). As the cherubim are very close to the thrones, God is represented as seated upon the cherubim by reason of their equality with the others. For in the eternal city each one of the angelic orders has its particular distinctions, which yet are common to the others. So, what each enjoys in a particular way is the undiminished property of the other orders also. But all the orders are not given the same name, for each is to be designated by the name of the peculiar ministry which it more specifically fulfills. So we said that seraphim signifies fire, but yet all the angels burn with the love of their Creator. The cherubim represent the fullness of knowledge, and yet of what is any angel ignorant, in that very place where together they see God, the source of all knowledge? The thrones are those in the midst of whom the Creator reigns, but none can enjoy eternal happiness, unless his Creator reigns within him. Therefore, what is in fact the property of all is attributed especially to those who receive it as a specific office to discharge. For if there is anything in some which the others cannot have, as in those properly called dominations and powers, all belongs to each, because through the charity of the spirit, each one enjoys whatever the others have.

But now, speaking of the angels, we have wandered far from our exposition of the Gospel. We must aspire to their happiness, but now let us return to ourselves. Let us remember that we are flesh and blood, and postpone our talk of the heavenly secrets until our penance wipes away the dust which makes us unclean in the sight of our Creator. Divine mercy promises us: "There shall be joy in heaven upon one sinner that doth penance," and by the prophet Ezechiel: "The justice of the just shall not deliver him in what day soever he shall sin" (Ezech. 33:12). Let us reflect as far as we may on this conduct of the divine mercy. He menaces the good with punishment should they fall, while he promises the sinners mercy in order that they may take courage to rise. He terrifies the first lest they become presumptuous in their good works; he encourages and animates the second, lest they despair in their sins. Are you good? Fear God's wrath that you may not fall. Are you a sinner? Put your trust in the divine mercy which will help you to rise. Consider that we are already fallen, that if left unaided we are utterly unable to rise, that we lie prostrate in the midst of our evil desires. But he who threatens to overthrow us if we are just, now stimulates us to overcome the sins which we have committed. He opens the bosom of his mercy, and invites us to go to him through penance. But we cannot do penance properly if we do not know how it should be done. To do penance truly is to lament those sins we have committed, and not to commit what we should lament. But he who weeps for his fault and at the same time commits another does not do penance: either he deceives himself, or else he does not know what penance is. Of what use is it to a man to repent of his sins of lust, if at the same time he is consumed by avarice? Or what benefit, if he bewail his faults of anger, when he allows himself to be dominated by envy? Therefore in order to do penance properly, we must not only repent of the evil we have committed but also refrain from committing further lamentable deeds: not only weep for our vices, but also fear to gratify them.

He who remembers his unlawful deeds should make an effort to abstain from what is lawful, as satisfaction to his Creator. He who enjoyed what is forbidden should likewise restrain himself from what is permissible, and mortify himself in small things when he knows that he has erred in big things. But all that I am saying now would be worthless, if it were not borne out by Holy Scripture. It is a fact that the law of the Old Testament forbade the coveting of another's wife (Exod. 20:17), but it did not forbid under any penalty that a king should order his soldiers to do difficult things or that a man should not drink water. We all know that David, overcome by his concupiscence, coveted and took the wife of another (2 Kgs. 11). This fault was followed by due punishment, and he amended it by penance. But later, when he faced the enemy troops, he longed to satisfy his thirst from a cistern at Bethlehem. Three brave soldiers, breaking through the enemy lines without suffering any hurt, brought the coveted water to their king. But he, having learned from his chastisement, immediately rebuked himself for having desired that water which had put his men in peril, and pouring it out upon the ground, he offered it to God, as it is written: "He would not drink, but offered it to the Lord" (2 Kgs. 23:16). The spilt water thus became a sacrifice made to God, for he atoned for the guilt of his concupiscence by the penance of his self-rebuke. So the man who formerly did not fear to covet the wife of another, later was afraid of having wished for water. Remembering the unlawful thing he had done, he restricted himself austerely from what was lawful. We are truly penitent when we deplore those sins we have committed. Let us think of the great indulgence of our Creator, who saw us sin and bore with us.

He who, before we fall, forbids us to sin, does not shut the doors of pardon on us, once we have committed it. See that he whom we despise calls upon us. We turn from him, but he does not turn from us. So that Isaias tells us:

"And thy eyes shall see thy teacher. And thy ears shall hear the word of one admonishing thee behind thy back" (Isa. 30:20–21). Man is, as it were, defended in front when, born in justice, he receives the commandments of up-righteous-ness. But when he despised those precepts, it was as if he turned his back upon his Maker. Yet see how he follows us; and though we have despised him, he does not cease to call us back. We turn our backs on him, with contempt for his words, treading on his laws: but even then he calls us yet again through his precepts, and waits for us in patience. Think, brethren, whether if any of you were speaking to your servant and he should turn his back proudly upon you: would you, his master, fail to punish him severely for such contempt? But when we sinned we turned away from our Creator, and still he tolerates us. He gently calls us from our pride, and although he could strike us as his enemies, instead he promises a reward on our return. Let such mercy on God's part melt the harshness of our guilty hearts; let man, who might have been severely punished for the evil he has done, at least feel shame at seeing the love with which God awaits his repentance.

XI.

The Rich Man and Lazarus

HOMILIA XL IN EVANGELIA

There was a certain rich man who was clothed in purple and fine linen and feasted sumptuously every day. And there was a certain beggar, named Lazarus who lay at his gate, full of sores, desiring to be filled with the crumbs that fell from the rich man's table. And no one did give him, moreover the dogs came and licked his sores. And it came to pass that the beggar died and was carried by the angels into Abraham's bosom. And the rich man also died; and he was buried in hell. And, lifting up his eyes when he was in torments, he saw Abraham afar off and Lazarus in his bosom; and he cried and said: Father Abraham, have mercy on me and send Lazarus, that he may dip the tip of his finger in water to cool my tongue; for I am tormented in this flame. And Abraham said to him: Son, remember that thou didst receive good things in thy lifetime, and likewise Lazarus evil things; but now he is comforted and thou art tormented. And besides all this, between us and you, there is fixed a great chaos; so that they who would pass from hence to you cannot, nor from thence come hither. And he said: Then, father, I beseech thee that thou wouldst send him to my father's house, for I have five brethren, that he may testify unto them, lest they also come into this place of torments. And Abraham said to him: They have Moses and the prophets. Let them hear them. But he said: No, father Abraham; but, if one went to them from the dead, they will do penance. And he said to him: If they hear not Moses and the prophets, neither will they believe if one rise again from the dead. (LUKE 16:19–31)

IN DEALING with the words of the holy Gospel, my dear brethren, it is necessary first to expound the historical truth, and afterwards to deduce the spiritual meaning of the allegory. The fruit of the allegory is more easily grasped, the more firmly the narrative is situated within the framework of its historical background. But since often the allegory strengthens our faith, while the historical aspect relates to morals, and since, by the grace of God, we are speaking to believers, there is reason to think that we may invert the order just indicated, and deal first with the allegorical sense of today's Gospel. But because its moral is also necessary for you, we shall treat of it at the end, as often one remembers more easily what one has heard more recently.

We shall treat as briefly as possible of the allegorical meaning of this passage, the more quickly to arrive at a full exposition of the moral considerations. "There was a certain rich man who was clothed in purple and fine linen and feasted sumptuously every day." Whom does this rich man represent, this man so richly dressed, who enjoyed all those daily banquets? Is it not the Jewish people, who made a cult of exterior things, using the delights of the law which they had received, for vain motives, not for true profit? And whom does Lazarus signify, covered in wounds, if not the Gentile peoples? These, when converted to God, were not ashamed to confess their sins, that is to say, they had many wounds and open sores. As when some infection comes from within the body to ulcers of the skin, so showing itself exteriorly, so when we confess our sins, it is in a sense an outbreak of our sores. In confession we manifest in a very profitable way the virus of sin which had concealed its venom within the soul. Exterior wounds bring to the surface the festering sore beneath, and when we confess our sins, we uncover this hidden sore. But the unfortunate Lazarus wished only to eat of the crumbs that fell from the rich man's table, and no one would give him any, because those proud people disdained to admit the Gentiles to the knowledge of their law. He who has knowledge of the truth and grows in conceit rather than in charity, swells and festers, as it were, with the riches he has been given. And, as the Jewish people had received these words of knowledge in abundance, they fell as crumbs from their table. But on the contrary, the dogs came and licked the ulcers of the poor man as he lay on the ground. Sometimes in Holy Scripture the word "dog" is used to mean a preacher. For dogs, when they lick wounds, cure them: thus when the holy doctors instruct us in the confession of our sins, we may say that they touch the ulcer of our mind with their tongue. When they exhort us, they deliver us from sin, as if restoring us to health. God himself tells us through the psalmist that the tongue of the preacher is signified by the word "dog," when he says: "The blood of thy enemies; the tongue of thy dogs be red with the same" (Ps. 67:24). From among the unfaithful Jews those holy preachers were chosen who, if I may use the expression, howled in the assertion of the truth, God's watchdogs against thieves and robbers. On the contrary, speaking of the rejection of some, we read: "Dumb dogs not able to bark" (Isa. 56:10). By the very fact that the holy preachers condemn sin, they approve its confession, saying "Confess therefore your sins one to another; and pray one for another, that you may be saved" (James 5:16). The dogs lick the wounds of Lazarus. Thus the holy doctors, when they receive the confession of the gentiles, cure the wounds of their soul. So that the name Lazarus is aptly interpreted as meaning "Helped," in that he is helped to recover by their correction and admonitions. By the licking of dogs one might also understand the smooth tongue of flatterers. For these lick our wounds when, as often happens, they praise us with despicable adulations for those very actions which our conscience tells us to be evil.

It happens, then, that both of these men die. The rich man, who wore purple and fine linen, is buried in hell. Lazarus is carried by the angels to Abraham's bosom. What does this phrase mean, if not the eternal repose reserved for the fathers? Speaking of this repose Christ tells us: "Many shall come from the east and the west, and shall sit down with Abraham and Isaac and Jacob in the kingdom of heaven; but the children of the kingdom shall be cast out into the exterior darkness" (Matt. 8:2). Thus he who was clad in purple and fine linen had reason to be called a child of the kingdom. This man lifted up his eyes from far off and saw Lazarus: for before the day of the last judgment, while the wicked are in hell, in the pains of their condemnation, they are able to see some of the faithful in their glory. This will be impossible after the last day. But what they see is indeed far off from them because, through lack of merit, they are unable to approach it. It is their tongue which suffers most; we see that from the holy Gospel, for the soul says: "Send Lazarus, that he may dip the tip of his finger in water to cool my tongue; for I am tormented in this flame." The unfaithful people had upon their lips the words of that law which they chose not to fulfill. So that member will burn the more, which would not put its knowledge into effect. So Solomon says of those who are instructed but negligent: "All the labor of man is for his mouth: but his soul shall not be filled" (Eccl. 6:7) for he who labors only to know what he ought to speak, derives no sustenance from his knowledge, which should be food for his soul. He wishes to be touched with the tip of the other's finger, since the soul condemned to everlasting fire longs to share in the actions, even the least, of the just. He will be told that he received his reward in this world, for he considered the enjoyment of transient pleasures as his supreme good. For the just can, and do, possess the goods of this world, but not as a reward, since they seek those which are better, that is to say, eternal. In their estimation, as they burn with the desire of heaven, earthly goods seem of little moment.

So that the prophet David, who enjoyed the riches and honors of a kingdom, although he considered these benefits as good, yet aspired ardently to one good only, saying: "It is good for me to adhere to my God" (Ps. 72:28). And we should remember what is said to him: "Son, remember." Notice that Abraham calls him son, even though he does not free him from his torments; for the fathers, faithful predecessors of that unfaithful people, seeing so many betrayed their faith, had no compassion whatsoever on them; nor did they release from pain those whom they recognized as their descendants according to the flesh. The rich man, in the midst of sufferings, says that he has five brothers: for that proud Jewish race, already for the greater part under sentence of condemnation, saw the followers whom they had left behind them upon earth given over to the satisfaction of the five corporal senses. So the number five is used to express the brothers he had left; for, plunged in hell, he bewails the lot of those whom he cannot return to warn, and he asks that Lazarus be sent. He is told, however, that they already have Moses and the prophets. But he says that they will not believe unless one go to them from the dead. The reply is immediate: "If they hear not Moses and the prophets, neither will they believe if one rise again from the dead." Speaking of Moses, Christ tells us: "If you did believe Moses, you would perhaps believe me also; for he wrote of me" (John 5:46). And Abraham's reply to the damned soul was fulfilled in regard to Jesus' resurrection. Our Lord rose from the dead, but the Jewish people, who would not believe Moses, also refused to believe him who rose from the dead. As they refused to understand the spiritual sense of Moses' words, they could not know him of whom Moses spoke.

Now that we have considered, dearly beloved, the hidden significance of the allegory, it remains to understand, in a broader fashion, the moral it contains. "There was a certain rich man who was clothed in purple and fine linen and feasted sumptuously every day. And there was a certain beggar, named Lazarus, who lay at his gate, full of sores." Some think that the precepts of the Old Testament were stricter than those of the new: but this is a grave mistake.

In the former robbery is condemned, and what has been taken unjustly must be repaid fourfold (2 Kgs. 12:4–6). But in the New, the rich man is rebuked for failing to give of his own, not for robbing others; not for doing violence to any man, but for being attached to his goods. So we can imagine what an enormous penalty will be imposed on the man who steals another's goods, when he who selfishly retains his own is sent to hell. Let no one consider himself secure, thinking: "I do no theft to others, but enjoy licitly the goods I have been given": not for robbing others, but for wickedly reserving for himself alone the wealth he had rightfully received, was this rich man condemned to hell. That is what brought about his condemnation: because he did not hesitate to seek only his own pleasure, because he used the possessions he had in the service of his pride, because he did not know the meaning of charity, because he did not attempt to redeem his sins with the riches which he had in such abundance. There are some who do not consider it a sin to love fine and expensive clothes. But if it were not a fault, our Lord would not have expressed so concisely the fact that the rich man, who was tormented in hell, had dressed while on earth in purple and fine linen. No one desires costly clothes, unless he is moved by ambition for earthly glory, that he may appear to excel others. That extravagant clothes are sought exclusively for this reason of vainglory is apparent from the fact that no one wishes to dress elegantly in a place where there is no one to see him. This fault will be seen more clearly, if we consider its opposite. If there were not virtue in humble dress, the evangelist would not have noted so minutely of John the Baptist that "he had his garment of camels' hair" (Matt. 3:4). But we should notice with close attention the order of narration which Christ observes in telling us of the proud man and the humble beggar. For he says: "There was a certain rich man," and immediately he adds: "and there was a certain beggar, named Lazarus." Among men it is common that the names of the rich should be known more widely than those of the poor. When our Lord, speaking of the rich man and the poor, tells us the name of the latter and not of the former, does not this fact show that God knows and approves of the humble, and is a stranger to the proud? So that, to many of those who pride themselves on their power to work miracles, God's final word will be: "I never knew you; depart from me, you that work iniquity" (Matt. 7:23). And on the other hand, God says to Moses: "I know thee by name" (Exod. 33:12). He says, then, of the rich man: "A certain man" and of the poor: "A beggar, named Lazarus." As if he were to say: "I know the poor man who is humble, I do not know the rich man who is proud. I know the former, because I approve his works; the latter I do not know in consequence of his wickedness."

We must also remember, brethren, the dispensations

of God's providence. A thing is done at times for more than one reason. Consider Lazarus, full of ulcers, as he lies at the rich man's gate. From this single circumstance, two judgments are derived. The rich man might have had some excuse if Lazarus, poor and ailing, had not lain there at his gate, if he had been far removed from him, if the sight of his need had not been constantly before his eyes. Again, if the rich man had not passed before him daily, the temptation of the beggar would have been greatly diminished and he would have suffered less. But since providence placed that needy sufferer before the gate of a man abounding in riches and delights, its plan achieved two things: the supreme condemnation for him who did not pity the beggar although he saw him, and the trial of the latter by his daily nearness to the other's wealth. How many inner temptations must have assailed him, poor, ill and in want, seeing that contrast with the other's health, enjoyments of comfort and of pleasure? He was pierced by pain and cold, while he saw the other dressed in fine clothes; he was oppressed by wounds while the other wasted the goods he had received; he had nothing, and the other gave him nothing. We cannot imagine how great his ordeal must have been, brethren, when his poverty alone would have been a great affliction, even had he enjoyed good health: or when his infirmity would have been sufficient hardship, even had he had plentiful riches! But so that his trial might be more searching, he was afflicted both with illness and with poverty, seeing the rich man leave his house surrounded by his army of servants, while no one visited him in his disease and want. This is evident from the fact that the dogs were free to lick his sores. So almighty God, by allowing Lazarus to lie before the rich man's door, formed two judgments: the rich man increased the punishment of his condemnation and the poor beggar, tried by temptation, received a greater reward. He looked down constantly on him for whom he had no pity and on him whom he was trying. On earth, two hearts: above, one searching them who, by proving one, was preparing him for glory, and by tolerating the other was preparing his punishment.

"And it came to pass that the beggar died and was carried by the angels into Abraham's bosom. And the rich man also died; and he was buried in hell." Now the rich man, from the middle of those flames, seeks a protector in him for whom he had no pity while on earth. "And, lifting up his eyes when he was in torments, he saw Abraham afar off and Lazarus in his bosom; and he cried and said: Father Abraham, have mercy on me and send Lazarus, that he may dip the tip of his finger in water to cool my tongue; for I am tormented in this flame." How unsearchable are the judgments of God, and how just the retribution he makes for good or evil actions! Earlier we were told that, while he was on earth, Lazarus longed for the crumbs that fell from the rich man's table, and no one would give him any. Now, we are told that the rich man in his agony desired that Lazarus dip one finger in water, that a drop might cool his mouth. Learn from this, brethren, how strict is the severity of God. The rich man who was unwilling to give the beggar the least morsel from his table, now in hell, pleads for equally trivial things. Now he cries for a drop of water, who denied a crumb of bread. We must, then, see the reason why the rich man asks for a drop of water to cool his tongue. In sacred Scripture we often find that one thing is related in order to clarify some other point. We saw that when our Lord spoke of the wealthy libertine, he did not say that he was very talkative, but that he was given to feastings. Nor does he say that he ever sinned through loquacity, but only through conceit and greed. But he who makes frequent festival is generally very talkative: so this man, who carried his merrymaking to excess in this life, condemned to flames, found that his tongue burned more than any other member. The first fault which follows intemperance in eating is usually verbosity, and second comes a tendency to sensuality. That this longing for play follows on voracity, we are shown by holy Scripture which tells us: "The people sat down to eat, and drink, and they rose up to play" (Exod. 32:6). But, before the body is inclined to play, the tongue is inclined to jesting and vain words. So when we are told that the rich man sought refreshment for his tongue, this must mean that he who feasted sumptuously sinned mainly through loquacity, and justly suffered a special torment in his tongue.

But we should reflect, with great fear, on Abraham's reply: "Son, remember that thou didst receive good things in thy lifetime, and likewise Lazarus evil things; but now he is comforted and thou art tormented." This sentence, brethren, hardly requires explanation: it is sufficient in itself to inspire terror. If some among you have received good things on earth, they should make you tremble, lest they be given you as recompense for some of your good actions; lest the judge, who here makes payment in external riches, should there withhold from you those goods which last; lest this world's honors and riches be the reward of your labor, when they should be an aid for your virtue. So when it is said: "Thou didst receive good things in thy lifetime," we understand that the rich man had received wealth on earth in return for some good actions he had done. Again, when we are told that Lazarus had received evil things, it is evident that he had done some evil actions, which had to be atoned for. But the fire of his penury purged Lazarus' wicked actions, while the good works of the rich man were paid with the transient happiness of this world. The first was oppressed and purified by poverty: the second was rewarded but perverted by his riches. Therefore, you who do good actions here on earth, when you receive wealth, be suspicious of it, lest that prosperity given you turn out to be the reward of those good deeds. And when you see some beggar do something bad, do not despise him, do not despair of him: perhaps the fire of his poverty purges and cleanses the stains of his guilt. But fear for yourselves: for it also happens that a prosperous life follows upon wicked deeds. And be solicitous for those others: for the poverty which torments them also leads them in the way of righteousness.

The Gospel continues: "And besides all this, between us and you, there is fixed a great chaos; so that they who would pass from hence to you cannot, nor from thence come hither." We must ponder these words: "They who would pass from hence to you cannot." For there is no doubt that those who are in hell long to enjoy the lot of the blessed. But since the latter have been received into eternal happiness, how can it be said that they desire to pass over to those who suffer in hell? It must be that, as the damned desire to go to the dwelling of the elect, to escape from that place of suffering, so the just wish to cross over in mercy to that place of torments, to bring them the freedom they desire. But those who wish to cross from heaven to hell can never do so; for although the souls of the just are aflame with mercy, nevertheless they are so united to the divine justice and guided always by rectitude, that they are not moved by any compassion towards the reprobate. They are in complete conformity with that judge to whom they are united, and so they cannot have compassion for those whom they cannot free from hell. They consider them as strangers, remote from themselves, since they have seen them repelled by their Maker who is the object of their own love. So neither the wicked can cross over to the felicity of the blessed: because they are shackled by an irrevocable condemnation, nor the just go to the unjust: because they cannot feel compassion for them whom the divine justice has rejected.

But now that this selfish tormented soul has been denied all hope of help, he remembers the brothers he has left on earth. At times, although to no purpose, the sufferings of the damned inspire a certain charity in them, to the point of having spiritual love for those whom, through attachment to sin, they did not love while on earth. So now he adds: "Then, father, I beseech thee that thou wouldst send him to my father's house, for I have five brethren, that he may testify unto them, lest they also come into this place of torments." Here we should note the ways in which the sufferings of the condemned man are increased. For his greater distress, he retains understanding and memory. He knows Lazarus, whom he despised, and he remembers his brothers, whom he left in the world. The punishment for his treatment of the beggar would not be complete, if he did not see him in the enjoyment of his unfading recompense. And he would not know perfect agony amid the flames, were he not tortured by the fear that his brothers might soon share that penalty. So for the greater punishment of sinners they will see the glory of those whom they once despised, and they will be tormented by the sufferings of those whom they loved in a useless way. It is believed that, before the day of judgment, the damned see some of the just in their glory so that, seeing their happiness, their own pains are increased by the vision of that everlasting joy.

Abraham gives an immediate reply to this request that Lazarus should be sent: "They have Moses and the prophets. Let them hear them." But he who refused to listen to the word of God, did not think his associates on earth could hear it either, so that he answers: "No, father Abraham, but if one went to them from the dead, they will do penance." However, he is answered truly: "If they hear not Moses and the prophets, neither will they believe if one rise again from the dead." Certainly, those who despised the words of the law, will scarcely fulfill the precepts of the risen Redeemer, so much more exacting. For the precepts of the old law are much easier than those of the new (Deut. 12). The former ordered tithes to be offered, but our Lord requires that those who seek perfection should abandon all (Luke 14). The old law condemns sins of the flesh, but he condemns even illicit thoughts. "If they hear not Moses and the prophets, neither will they believe if one rise again from the dead." For how can those who neglect to fulfill the milder dictates of the old law obey the stricter commands of the risen Christ? And it is evident that, if they refuse to carry out what they are told, they withhold also their belief. We have now said sufficient for our consideration of the Gospel.

My dear brethren, now that you know the glory of Lazarus and the punishment of the rich man, act with extreme caution; seek out the poor, that in the day of judgment they may be your intercessors and advocates. You have many brothers of Lazarus lying at your doors, in want of those crumbs which fall daily from your table when you have well satisfied your appetite. The words we have been reading should teach us to fulfill the law of mercy. Every minute we find a Lazarus if we seek him, and every day without seeking we find one at our door. Now beggars besiege us, imploring alms; later they will be our advocates. Rather it is we who should beg, and yet we are besought. Ask yourselves whether we should refuse what we are asked, when those who ask us are our patrons.

Therefore do not lose the opportunity of doing works of mercy; do not store unused the good things you possess. Before punishment is inflicted, think on it. When you see poor people in this world, do not despise them, even if you see defects in them, for it may be that their wounds, inflicted by vicious habits, are cured by the medicine of poverty. If, in any of these poor people, you see something which merits rebuke, certainly do so with the object of gaining greater merit, so that your mercy is more generous as their vices are more abundant. At the same time as you give the reprimand, give them bread: the bread to nourish them and the reprimand to correct them, so that they who sought only one obtain two nourishments from you: bodily food and interior counsel. So when a poor person is found at fault, he should be admonished, but never despised. If he has no fault, he should have our highest respect, as our intercessor. But we see many poor persons of whose merit we are wholly ignorant. So all are worthy of our veneration, and we must humble ourselves before all, since we do not know which among them may be Christ.

I am going to tell you something, brethren, all the details of which my brother and fellow-priest Speciosus, here present, can vouch for. In the same year as I entered the monastery, there lived in this city, near the church of the blessed Virgin Mary, a certain old woman named Redempta, who had taken the religious habit.[†] She had been a disciple of that Herundina who was said to have lived as a hermit in the Praenestine mountains, and who was famed for her great virtue. Redempta had two disciples living with her, and they wore the same habit as she. One was called Romula and the other is still alive: I know her to see, but I do not know her name. These three women lived together in the

---

†   Cf. *Dialogues*, book IV, chap. 15.

same house and although they had riches at their disposal, they lived a life of poverty in all things. However, Romula behaved in a much more meritorious way than her companion. She was a model of patience and obedience, scrupulous in her observance of silence, and ardently given to prayer. But it often happens that those whom men consider perfect, yet retain some imperfection in the eyes of the supreme Artist. The same thing happens when, unskilled in art, we see some statue has yet uncompleted which we think is perfect, and praise it as if it were a finished work. In spite of the praise he hears, the sculptor continues to chisel and too polish it, in order to achieve perfection. So this Romula of whom we are speaking was stricken by an infirmity which doctors call paralysis: this kept her in bed for many years, depriving her of the use of her limbs. But none of her sufferings could move her to impatience. In her the loss of her limbs meant increase of virtue, for she exercised herself all the more in prayer seeing that she was incapable of other action. One night she called Redempta, who looked after her disciples as if they were her daughters, and she said to her: "Come, mother; come". Her other companion soon joined Redempta, as did other persons also, to hear Romula repeating the same words. I myself heard of it at that time. At midnight, when Redempta and her other disciple were beside the sick-bed, suddenly a heavenly light filled the whole room, of such clarity and splendor that the hearts of those who saw it were seized with a great terror and, as they later recounted, their bodies became as if petrified, and they stood as if in a profound stupor. And a great noise was heard, as of a passing multitude, and a knocking on the doors of the room, as if a crowd were entering, jostling one another. According to their account, they felt that a multitude was entering, but because of their fear and the intense brilliance of the light, they could not see anything. They shut their eyes for fear, blinded by the radiance of the light. A delightful perfume soon followed that light, so that their soul, seemingly drowned in brilliance, was revived by this fragrance. But, as they could not bear that dazzling beam, Romula herself began gently to console her mistress Redempta, trembling beside the bed. "Do not fear, mother," she said. "I am not dying yet." Immediately she said these words, the light disappeared, but the fragrance remained for the space of three days. On the fourth night, once more she called her mistress, asking her that the Viaticum should be given her, and this was done. Redempta and the other had not as yet drawn near the invalid, when suddenly there appeared in the street, before the door of the house in which they were, two choirs which chanted the psalms. As the two women told us, they could hear voices of men and women: the men singing the psalms, and the women answering. As soon as these celestial obsequies began outside the sickroom, that saintly soul was freed from the body and was taken up into its glory. According as the choirs of singers ascended, leading her to heaven, their psalmody grew more indistinct, until the sound of the singers and the fragrance of perfume died away completely.

While this woman was in the world, what honors did she receive? She seemed unworthy of notice, despised by all. Who would have troubled to visit or approach her? But in that refuse-heap, there lay a pearl of God. I call that terrible poverty and that corruption of the body a refuse-heap. But the pearl which lay in it was raised up and set among the jewels of the divine king: now it shines with the citizens of heaven, brilliant as any precious stone in the eternal diadem. Oh you, who think you possess the riches this world, or who do possess them, compare, if you can, that false wealth of yours with the lasting treasures of Romula. You will have to leave all your possessions here; she sought nothing on her way, and found everything at the end of her journey. You lead a pleasant life but you fear an unhappy death: she bore the distresses of this life, but ended it in rapture. You seek the temporal adulation of men: she, despised by men, found fellowship among the angels.

Learn, brethren, to despise all the things of earth; scorn all transient honors and seek the glory which endures. Respect all the poor you meet, and when you see them ignored by the world, treat them as friends of God. Share your riches with them, so that they, in their turn, may share theirs with you. Remember what has been said by the apostle of the Gentiles: "In this present time let your abundance supply their want, that their abundance also may supply your want" (2 Cor. 8:14). Remember also Christ's words: "As long as you did it to one of these my least brethren, you did it to me" (Matt. 25:40). Why, then, are you slow to give, when everything you give to the poor man here on earth, you give to him who is in heaven? But may almighty God, who speaks to you through me, impress these truths upon your minds, God who lives and reigns with the Father, in the unity of the Holy Ghost, world without end. Amen.

XII.

The Good Shepherd

HOMILIA XIV IN EVANGELIA

I am the good shepherd. The good shepherd giveth his life for his sheep. But the hireling, and he that is not the shepherd, whose own the sheep are not, seeth the wolf coming and leaveth the sheep and flieth; and the wolf catcheth and scattereth the sheep. And the hireling flieth, because he is a hireling; and he hath no care for the sheep. I am the good shepherd; and I know mine, and mine know me. As the Father knoweth me, and I know the Father; and I lay down my life for my sheep. And other sheep I have that are not of this fold; them also I must bring. And they shall hear my voice; and there shall be one fold and one shepherd. (JOHN 10:11–16)

IN TODAY'S Gospel, dearly beloved brethren, you have heard something which adds greatly to your instruction, and to my peril. For you see that he who is good in essence, and not by any mere accident, says: "I am the good shepherd." And he adds the quality of his goodness which we should imitate. "The good shepherd giveth his life for his sheep." The Lord followed his own counsel and fulfilled his own command. As a good shepherd he gave his life for his sheep, to the point of giving, in the sacrament of the altar, his body and blood to be the food of those he had redeemed. We are shown the path we must pursue, without fear of death: we see the model we must imitate. Firstly, we must use all our exterior assets in the service of those sheep, and then, if necessary, we must give our lives for them. Through the former requirement, which is the lesser, we reach the latter, which is the greater. As life itself is dearer to us than all external possessions, how will he give his life for his sheep, who will not give them lesser things? There are some who love wealth more than their sheep, who have no right to be called pastors. Of these our Lord says: "The hireling, and he that is not the shepherd, whose own the sheep are not, seeth the wolf coming and leaveth the sheep and flieth; and the wolf catcheth and scattereth the sheep."

He is called a hireling, and not a pastor, who gives grazing to God's sheep for love of gain and not for any love of them. He is a hireling who occupies the place of a pastor, but does not seek the betterment of those who are his subjects. He desires worldly comforts, taking pleasure in the pride of his position: he pastures the sheep solely for the sake of temporal reward, and is gratified by the esteem of men. For these are the rewards of the hirelings. Here they find what they seek in payment for their labors, but hereafter they are excluded from the inheritance enjoyed by the flock. Except in very exceptional cases we cannot know the true pastor from the hireling; for in time of peace and tranquility the sheep are guarded by the hireling with the same fidelity, it seems, as the shepherd. However, the approach of the wolf is sufficient to indicate the motives of each. The wolf descends upon the sheep when any unjust or predatory person oppresses the faithful and persecutes the humble. But that man who seemed to be a shepherd, but is a hireling, abandons the sheep and flees; because when he sees danger to himself, he will not oppose injustice. He flees, not physically, but by refusing to give consolation. He flees when he sees injustice and is silent; he flees when he hides behind his silence. Of all such people, God has said through the prophet Ezechiel: "You have not gone up to face the enemy, nor have you set up a wall for the house of Israel, to stand in battle in the day of the Lord" (Ezech. 13:5). To go up to face the enemy means to uphold rightful liberty in the face of any powers which oppress. We stand firm in battle for the house of Israel, raising a wall around it in the Lord's day, if with all the strength of justice we defend the innocent faithful against the injustice of the wicked. Since the hireling does none of this when he sees the wolf, we can say that he flees.

There is another kind of wolf, the type which ravages

the mind, rather than the body. These are the evil spirits, which continually surround the sheepfold of the faithful, seeking the death of their souls. Of this wolf, Christ says: "And the wolf catcheth and scattereth the sheep." The wolf comes, and the hireling flees, when the evil spirit tortures the mind of the faithful with temptation, and he who holds the place of pastor has no true concern for them. Souls perish, while he dallies with worldly consolations. The wolf catches and scatters the sheep, when he entices one to lust, another to avarice, inflates one with pride and sears another with anger, rouses this man to envy, traps that into falsehood. As the wolf scatters and kills the flock, so the devil overruns the faithful by temptation. But the hireling is not inflamed with zeal, burns with no fire of love: as he seeks only external comforts, he remains indifferent to the spiritual loss of his flock. So Christ continues: "The hireling flieth, because he is a hireling; and he hath no care for the sheep." The only reason why the hireling runs away is that he is a hireling. As if to say clearly: He cannot stand firm when peril threatens the sheep because, in caring for them, he seeks only temporal profit and has no love for them. Esteeming honor, rejoicing in temporal goods, he is afraid to face danger, lest he lose those comforts which he loves. As our Redeemer notes the weakness of the false shepherd, again he shows us the model we must imitate: "I am the good shepherd." And he adds: "and I know mine," that is to say, I love them, "and mine know me," as if he meant: They follow those who love them. For he who does not love the truth does not yet know it.

Now, brethren, that you have considered the peril in which I stand, ask yourselves what danger to you is implied in the words of our Lord. Are you truly his sheep? Do you know him, realizing that he is the true light? Do you know him, not by faith alone, but by love: not by your assent only, but in your action? John the Evangelist gives testimony of this when he says: "He who saith that he knoweth him, and keepeth not his commandments, is a liar; and the truth is not in him" (1 John 2:4). So that in the Gospel, our Lord continues: "As the Father knoweth me, and I know the Father; and I lay down my life for my sheep." As if he said: "I know the Father and am known by him from the very fact of my laying down my life for my sheep; that is, it is by the charity with which I die for my sheep, that I show how much I love my Father." So that we might see that he came to redeem not only the Jews, but the Gentiles also, he adds: "And other sheep I have that are not of this fold; them also I must bring. And they shall hear my voice; and there shall be one fold and one shepherd." Our Lord had already provided for the redemption of us who come from Gentile stock, when he said that he brings other sheep. You see this, brethren, happen daily; you see the reconciliation of the Gentiles an accomplished fact today. Of two flocks he has made one, uniting the Jewish and Gentile peoples in belief in him. St. Paul bears witness of this when he says: "He is our peace, who hath made both one" (Eph. 2:14). Choosing the simple of heart from both peoples, he brought all sheep to the one fold.

Of these sheep, he says again: "My sheep hear my voice; and I know them; and they follow me. And I give them life everlasting" (John 10:27–28). And earlier he says: "By me, if any man enter in, he shall be saved; and he shall go in and go out, and shall find pastures" (John 10:9). He shall go in to faith, and shall go out from faith to vision, and find pasture in the eternal banquet. Therefore, his sheep find pasture: for all who are simple in heart follow him, and are nourished by the pasturage which is eternally green. What is the food of these sheep, if not the intimate joys of paradise? Their food is the countenance of God present before them, which, seen without any barriers, bestows lasting nourishment on the soul. They rejoice in the happiness of those eternal meadows, because they evaded the snares of carnal pleasure upon earth. There they hear the choirs of angels sing hymns, and enjoy the company of all the heavenly citizens. There is never-ending celebration for the glorious return of those who come from their dreary labor on earth. The ranks of the prophets exult; the apostles and the victorious army of martyrs rejoice, and their joy increases in accordance with the severity of their sufferings on earth.

There, the constancy of the confessors is rewarded; the faithful whom the allurements of vice could not seduce; the holy women who overcame the world and the weakness of their sex; children, whose saintliness outpaced their years; old men weakened by age, who yet conserved their spiritual strength.

Let us then, brethren, seek those pastures where we shall rejoice amid so many companions. Let that joy itself serve as a stimulus to our efforts. Certainly, if any town were celebrating some feast, or the dedication of a church, we should all make haste to meet together and attend. Each would try his best to do so, thinking himself unlucky if he could not be there. See what jubilation is manifest in heaven's streets, each rejoicing in the presence of the others; and yet we remain cold to the love of things which last, unkindled by desire, indifferent as to whether we attend. We deprive ourselves of happiness and still we are satisfied. Let us inflame our hearts, our faith in what we believe, our yearnings for the things of eternity. If we love thus, we shall go there. No adversity can deprive us of our interior bliss, because if anyone is truly determined to reach the eternal resting-place, no roughness in his path can alter that determination. No flattering prosperity must deceive us: that traveler is very foolish who, looking at the pleasant scenery around him, forgets to advance towards his journey's end. Therefore, let us long with all our heart to reach our enduring home. Let nothing of this world hold us back, since we know that very soon we must leave it all. Thus, if we are true sheep of the divine Shepherd, not dallying to feed on the pleasures of the way, we shall find a lasting food in unfading pastures.

Designed by Fiona Cecile Clarke, the Cluny Media *logo
depicts a monk at work in the scriptorium,
with a cat sitting at his feet.*

*The monk represents our mission to emulate
the invaluable contributions of the monks
of Cluny in preserving the libraries of the West,
our strivings to know and love the truth.*

*The cat at the monk's feet is Pangur Bán, from the
eponymous Irish poem of the 9th century.
The anonymous poet compares his scholarly
pursuit of truth with the cat's happy hunting of mice.
The depiction of Pangur Bán is an homage to the work
of the monks of Irish monasteries and a sign
of the joy we at Cluny take in our trade.*

"Messe ocus Pangur Bán,
cechtar nathar fria saindan:
bíth a menmasam fri seilgg,
mu memna céin im saincheirdd."

www.ingramcontent.com/pod-product-compliance
Lightning Source LLC
Chambersburg PA
CBHW070436100426
42812CB00031B/3306/J